Gdańsk - Past and Present

Bohdan Szermer

Gdańsk – Past and Present

INTERPRESS PUBLISHERS, WARSAW 1971

CONTENTS

PAST

AT THE MOUTH OF THE VISTULA

When you look for Gdańsk on the map, you can find a spot on the southern shore of the Baltic Sea where the winding line of the Vistula River meets the sea. "At the mouth of the Vistula" is how the location of Gdańsk is usually described. However, this description is not exactly correct — the waters of the Vistula discharge into the Baltic 18 kilometres to the east of Gdańsk and also within the city itself. Although part of it is called Wisłoujście, which means mouth of the Vistula, at present, it would be impossible to locate the river's mouth.

However, it is not a mistake to link the name Gdańsk with the river Vistula for it was to this most Polish of rivers that the city owes its foundation and prosperity. And, to go even further — the Vistula actually created some of the land on which the city and port of Gdańsk developed. In order to explain this fact, we must go back thousands of years, to the time when the last glaciers were retreating to the north, leaving behind them a landscape of moraines and lakes, including one great lake which later became the sea. During the last stage of the formation of the Baltic Sea, the southern coastline was much more varied, and a deep bay

reached as far as today's Tczew and Malbork. Winds, tides and sea waves, by creating sand-bars, began to cut off this bay from the sea, building up a sandy peninsula. At the same time, the Vistula deposited millions of tons of sand and alluvial soil which gradually began to fill in the bay, forming a low-lying delta known as Żuławy Wiślane. As in every delta, the river diverged into numerous branches which often changed their course and kept covering in other parts of the bay. It has been proved, for example, that during a certain period the lower course of the Motława, which today is a small river flowing through Gdańsk, was one of these branches.

In historical times, the Vistula had two main branches: the Nogat, which flowed to the northeast and the Leniwka, which flowed north and then turned west. Already at that time, the Motława discharged into the Leniwka, and the Leniwka's outlet to the sea was near Wisłoujście. It was in this region, where the Motława joined the Vistula, very near one of the Vistula mouths, that Gdańsk was founded.

The Vistula connected the city with its hinterland

Gdańsk — a city situated on the edge of the delta plain of the Vistula and a glacial level

so that goods could be transported to Gdańsk by river which became a rich trading port. However, this same Vistula carried with it alluvial soil which silted up the mouth, formed shoals and pushed the coastline further and further away, thus making navigation more and more difficult. The inhabitants of Gdańsk put much effort into maintaining the mouth of the river which, at the same time, was the entrance to their port, fit for navigation. If we also take into account the dangerous floods which occurred in these low-lying areas, it will become clear that the river had its disadvantages as well. Therefore, when in 1840 the Vistula, swollen with piled ice broke through the ridge of dunes, and formed a new mouth called Przełom Wisły or Wisła Śmiała, this was immediately made use of. The former branch of the river, cut off by floodgates, became the Martwa Wisła (Dead Vistula). Then the sea itself covered up the old mouth with sand.

Nothing was done to prevent this because a new entrance to the port had already been opened earlier. This was located about two kilometres to the west of the old mouth.

All these developments resulted in the fact that, in Gdańsk today, there is no mouth of the Vistula, although there is a place called Wisłoujście. In further chapters, we shall return to this somewhat involved question of access to Gdańsk port. However, the way the present mouth came into existence should be explained since Przełom Wisły is not the mouth of the Vistula either. When Przełom Wisły was formed, a few sharp turns in the river still existed, as did the menace of ice jams and, thus, of floods. This is why a canal was dug in the years 1890—1895, near the village of Świbno. It was seven kilometres long and carried the waters of the Vistula to the sea along the shortest route. A further part of the old river bed was cut off by floodgates and, thus, the Dead Vistula was lengthened. The city was thus fully protected against floods and the port against obstruction while retaining its access to the Vistula. As a result of these changes, Gdańsk had ceased to lie at the mouth of the Vistula, in the strict sense of the word.

But the Vistula is only one of the elements of the Gdańsk landscape. Others are its undulating upland, the sea, the beaches, the sand dunes on the seashore, and the Żuławy depression.

The Gdańsk upland is undoubtedly the most arresting feature of the local landscape. It owes its characteristic appearance to moraines which were deposited by glaciers and, later, sculptured by water flowing down them. The upland rises to a height of 40 to 50 metres in the southern and 100 to 150 metres in the northern part of the city and to as much as 150 to 200 metres further to the north and the west. It is strongly undulating, especially the north. In the east, it ends in an abrupt drop of ten metres high, and in Gdynia to the west, where the moraine hills reach the sea, in picturesque high cliffs. The part of the upland near the eastern edge is cut across by numerous valleys, the largest of which are the valley of the Oliwski Stream (part of which is known as Dolina Radości — Valley of Happiness) in Oliwa, the valley of the Strzyża, the valley formerly known as "royal" in Wrzeszcz, and the Siedlecka Valley which lies to the centre of Gdańsk.

The sheer drop of the edge of the upland and its varied profile give someone looking up from the valley the impression that he has real hills before him. These "hills," especially the part covered by forests, form one of the most characteristic and beautiful elements of the Gdańsk landscape. At the same time, however, they make it difficult for the city to expand and, to an extent, even set a limit to its growth. Among these "hills" there are two that deserve special mention. These are the elevations that rise on both sides of the mouth of the Siedlecka Valley, known as Grodzisko and Biskupia

Gdańsk owes its varied landscape to the action of the continental glacier, the Vistula accumulation, to the streams and winds.

ZATOKA GDAŃSKA

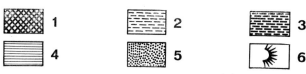

1. Post-glacial upland 2. Delta lowland 3. Depression — former lakes 4. Accumulation platform 5. Sand dunes on the seashore 6. Sandy taluses at the entrance of bigger valleys

From the west, the city is bordered by a strongly undulating upland. A part of the Siedlce district

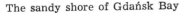

The sandy shore of Gdańsk Bay

Górka, which overlook the centre of Gdańsk in the west.

The second characteristic element of the Gdańsk landscape is the sea, or to be more exact — Gdańsk Bay. This is a complete contrast to the upland: a great flat expanse which reaches to the horizon, seemingly monotonous and uninteresting but, in reality, always changing, depending on the weather. When the visibility is good, one can see the faint line of the Hel Peninsula which shuts off the bay in the north, and turns it into a convenient roadstead for ships waiting to enter the port.

The sandy beaches, formed many ages ago in the shape of a great, regular bow, have now two bulges at Gdańsk, both created by the Vistula. One of them — in the west — is Nowy Port and Westerplatte, formed by sands deposited here by the Leniwka at her old mouth near Wisłoujście. The second bulge was created at Przełom Wisły at the time when it was the river mouth. The former coastline is still marked by sand dunes which are the remnants of older dunes and form two distinct lines: Czarny Dwór, Zaspa, Letnica, Stogi and Brzeźno, Nowy Port, Wisłoujście. This ridge of sand dunes is part of a former sand-bar which once cut off today's Żuławy when it was still a sea bay and which further east is known as the Mierzeja Wiślana (Vistula Sand-bar) and still cuts off the Zalew Wiślany (Vistula Lagoon) from the sea. This ridge is neither high nor wide in the north-west part, but it rises towards the east and within the city reaches a height of 20 metres above sea level at the Przełom Wisły. Some of the sand dunes are covered with forests and the rest are protected by special plants.

The dunes play an important role for they protect the delta depression, most of which lies below sea level (within Gdańsk up to 1.2 metres and in Żuławy 1.8 metres). Most of the land in the delta was formed on the site of the place of the former sea bay, by alluvial and other deposits. However, not the whole area was filled in this way. Some remaining

Fertile alluvial soil deposited by the Vistula form the vast delta plain — the Żuławy depression

lakes and pools gradually became overgrown and were finally drained only thanks to man's determined effort, some of them as long ago as the early Middle Ages. Dams, numerous canals, windmills once used to drain these areas, and the pumping stations that now force water from the canals into the rivers that run between the dikes above the level of the whole area, all these elements form a landscape that reminds one very much of Holland. These are excellent agricultural lands, but it is very difficult to build on them. They cover the whole eastern part of Gdańsk, reach the centre of town and extend to the edge of the upland south of the city centre. They also extend into lower Sopot in a long wedge adjacent to the sand dunes on the seashore.

To conclude this description of the natural features of Gdańsk, one should add that between the steep edge of the Gdańsk upland and the delta depression in Wrzeszcz, Oliwa and part of Sopot, there is an almost flat strip of land covered with sand and gravel which, in places, is as much as three kilometres wide. At the mouth of most of the valleys, especially the Siedlecka Valley, the flowing waters have formed sandy taluses. These areas, together with the slightly hilly parts of the upland, although less picturesque, are much more useful for building.

A THOUSAND YEARS AGO

In order to present the history of the people who lived in these areas, one must reach into the very distant past. Numerous findings testify that man lived in Gdańsk Pomerania as early as the Stone Age. Starting from the Bronze Age, it is possible to trace continuous settlement here, and also, within today's city of Gdańsk, especially in its southern part (Orunia, Święty Wojciech).

Archaeologists have shown that Gdańsk Pomerania was settled by Slavonic tribes about 3,000 years ago. Primitive ovens used to smelt iron, which were found near Gdańsk, date from 2,500 years ago. During the first centuries of our era, the Slavonic tribe of Veneti already sailed the Baltic. At the same time, numerous Roman and Arabian coins found in this area prove that there must have been a much frequented commercial route which led from the south of Europe, through the Moravian Gate and Kalisz, along the lower Vistula, towards the sea. This route was called the "amber trail" because of the amber found on the Baltic Coast which was one of the main objects of interest to Roman and Arabian merchants. The route which led from

the south reached the foot of the Gdańsk upland, between Biskupia Górka and Grodzisko, and the swamps on the Motława, then it turned to the north-west. Another road led through the Siedlecka Valley to the west. Many things found here, including coins, testify to still another commercial route which led along the Vistula Sand-bar toward the sands of Sambia, abounding with amber. The uneven terrain of the Gdańsk upland to the west which made travelling difficult, and the swamps and flood-waters of the delta to the east, were the reason why all these roads met between the mouth of the Siedlecka Valley and the marshes along the river, where the centre of Gdańsk is today.

During the years before the Polish state was formed, a large complex of settlements already existed here on the sites of today's towns of Pruszcz, Święty Wojciech, Otomin, Pręgowo, Chmielno, Oliwa, Sopot, Oksywie and Wejherowo. It is also possible that a fortified settlement existed in Grodzisko. Perhaps there was even a trade centre in the neighbourhood of today's Church of St Nicholas, that is, where the oldest trade routes met, near the cross-

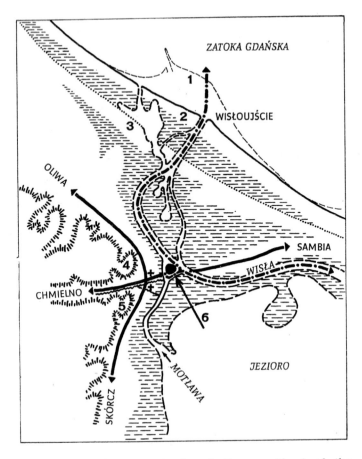

Steep slopes of the upland and the marshland of the Vistula Delta marked the course of the oldest trade routes. Near the place they crossed between the two branches of the Motława and Vistula, a castle-town of Gdańsk was founded. It guarded shipping trade on the Vistula, as well as the travel route to amber-rich Sambia.

1. Present coastline 2. Hypothetical coastline at the time when Gdańsk was founded 3. Former coastline 4. Grodzisko hill 5. Biskupia Górka 6. Castle-town of Gdańsk. Location of the oldest Gdańsk churches is marked by crosses

ing to the sand-bar and the road leading to Sambia.

Since information in those historical documents that have been preserved is scanty, there was speculation regarding the beginnings of Gdańsk and the earliest stage of its history, some of it quite controversial. After the Second World War, system-atic archaeological and other research, undertaken over a period for more than ten years, helped to solve many doubts. It was also possible to recreate a picture of the Gdańsk of the early Middle Ages, although some points are still unclear and certain hypotheses await confirmation.

Traces of a castle-town were discovered by archaeologists in the north-eastern part of the centre of the city, along Rycerska, Grodzka and Sukien-nicza streets. It was built on a swampy island, located between two branches of the Motława and the Vistula, which then ran along a different bed. The approximate date of the foundation of the town was estimated as the year 980. This was the period when Mieszko I organized the Polish state or, to be more exact, the period when he added Pomerania to his kingdom. Both this fact and the settlement's power-ful defensive (on an island) and strategic position (at the mouth of the Vistula) allow one to assume that the foundation of Gdańsk was connected with the consolidation of the rule of the first Polish monarch on the Baltic Coast. Gdańsk therefore is as old as the Polish state and, from its beginnings, has been connected with its thousand-year-long history.

The size of the island on which the castle-town was built was over two hectares and the settlement covered almost the entire area. Probably the shape of the island influenced the shape of the town; it was built in the form of an irregular oval or rather a triangle with markedly rounded points. The settle-ment was surrounded by a powerful rampart built of wood and earth. In a few places, it was strength-ened by wooden bastions. The construction of the external part of the rampart was of the hook type, typical of Slavonic castles. This rampart, which was 15 metres wide at the bottom and probably 10 me-tres high in places, served not only for defence. It also protected the interior of the town against flood-

Archaeological excavations have become an important source of information on Gdańsk of the early Middle Ages. Wooden construction from almost ten centuries ago has been clearly detected in the excavation

ing. To the south and west, along the two branches of the Motława, the wooden quays of the first Gdańsk port lay close to the external side of the rampart. On the Vistula side, the rampart was protected by a special breakwater.

The prince's seat was located in the eastern corner of the town. It took up one-fifth of the area of the town and was separated from the rest by an internal rampart. Apart from the royal quarters, there were rooms for the prince's guards and servants, stables and other ancillary buildings. There probably also existed a chapel in the settlement. The ap-

The Late Romanesque granite base with crockets uncovered in the wall of the house at 26 Mariacka Street (The Archaeological Museum), and similar bases from Artus Court and the Crane, may come from the chapel of the castle-town — probably the first brick building in Gdańsk

proach to the town from the west was by ferry or across a wooden bridge over the branch of the Motława and led through a gate in the external rampart across the western part of the castle-town through a second gate to the prince's seat. The western part of the town, where fishermen and artisans lived, consisted of wooden houses, usually built of whole logs from 4 by 4 metres to 10 by 5 metres in size. Archaeologists estimate that there were about 100 such houses. The streets were narrow, only 2 to 3 metres wide, with the exception of the main street, which was twice as wide. The number of inhabitants in this earliest period is placed at a thousand or somewhat more.

The first written mention of Gdańsk dates from the year 999 and comes from the "Life of St Adalbert" written in Rome. The passage that interests us refers to the year 997 when Adalbert, former bishop of Prague, sent by Bolesław the Brave to convert the Prussians, travelled through Gdańsk. For a few days he stayed in the city which belonged to the Polish state, and baptised many of its inhabitants. This account is of particular importance for three reasons. To begin with, it gives the written name of the town — GYDDANYZC — for the first time. Taking into consideration the difficulties of phonetic transcription this can be assumed to be a version of the city's present name. Secondly, the word *urbs* — "city" — was used in the quoted note to describe the town. This word, of course, had a different meaning in the early Middle Ages but it was only used to describe the largest towns. Still another detail is of great importance: the missionary expedition of Bishop Adalbert left Gdańsk by ship; the choice of Gdańsk as the starting point emphasizes the importance of the town and role as a port.

There is a lack of further written sources about the history of Gdańsk in the 11th and the first half of the 12th century. But archaeological excavations testify to its further development during the 11th century, until a great fire broke out which destroyed it towards the end of the century. We can assume that this catastrophe was connected with the riots which occurred in Pomerania during the reign of Władysław Herman. After a temporary decline caused by these events, a period of renewed development took place during the reign of Bolesław the Wrymouth. The town of Gdańsk was surrounded by new, more powerful ramparts made of earth and wood, and new streets were laid out within the town. The houses, still made of wood, were closer to each other and smaller, but some of them by then were two storeys.

After the death of Bolesław the Wrymouth in 1138, Poland entered into a period of feudal division into separate districts. At that time, Gdańsk Pomerania was under the rule of a local dynasty of princes. In 1186 Prince Sambor I brought in Cistercian monks who founded the monastery in Oliwa and around 1200 began to build a stone church, which is part of the present chancel. During the first half of the 13th century, a transept was added and some of the western portion constructed. The church was planned and built under the influence of Danish architecture; its style is transitional, between Romanesque and Gothic.

Probably at the turn of the 12th century, a large settlement grew up to the west of Gdańsk below the ramparts. It was bounded by today's Podwale Staromiejskie Street in the south; in the west by the present Podmłyńska Street and in the north by the Church of St Bridget and Zamkowa or Kumoszek Street. This settlement or *suburbium* had its own port which was located on a branch of the Motława, opposite the castle-town and, later, also near Podwale Staromiejskie or, at least, its eastern part.

Prince Świętopełk II (1220—1266) brought the order of Dominican friars from Cracow to Gdańsk and, during the 1230's, they built a new, stone church to replace the old Church of St Nicholas which was probably made of wood. Traces of this church were found beneath the floor of the south-eastern part of the present building. About the same time, the original Church of St Catherine was built as a new parish church. The market place was

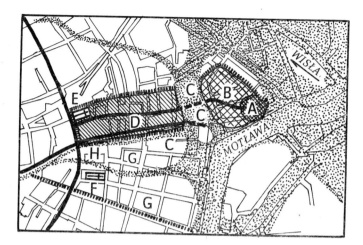

Early Medieval Gdańsk. This is how the layout of the town looked in the 13th century, according to Dr Andrzej Zbierski, based on excavated material. Drawing of the town (lines), castle-town (squares) and former outline of the Vistula and Motława Rivers (dots) is set on the present layout of streets. A. Prince's seat B. Castle-town C. Port D. Town since the beginning of the 13th century E. St. Catherine's Church F. St Nicholas' Church G. Areas belonging to the Dominican Friars H. Market Square

located at the crossing of the above-mentioned trade routes, between these two churches.

Both historical documents and excavations testify to the importance of the Gdańsk of those days as a trade centre. From their testimony, it appears that Gdańsk kept up trade relations with Flanders, England, Germany, Scandinavia, Bohemia, Hungary and Russia, and also with Italy and the Middle East. Apart from trade, handicrafts also developed and the first industrial enterprises were set up — mills, powered by the waters of the Siedlecki Stream or perhaps by canals dug specially for the purpose.

Świętopełk II granted Gdańsk a royal charter around 1240. In the years 1261 to 1263, Gdańsk also received a charter based on Lübeck law. It is difficult to explain this "double" granting of charters. Now it is considered almost certain that the Lübeck charter was granted to the new settlement established to the south of the church and on the grounds

Late Romanesque bases and charakteristic trapezoid capitals of semi-columns, shaped under Danish influence, have also been preserved in the southern aisle of the Cistercian Church in Oliwa; the aisle was built in the first half of the 13th century

belonging to the Dominicans, in the area of the present St Mary's Church and Długi Targ Street.

At any rate, toward the end of the 13th century Gdańsk was already a large town with an estimated population of eight to ten thousand inhabitants. Although a large number of settlers from western Europe, especially merchants, began to come here during this century, the population of Gdańsk was still, in the overwhelming majority, Slavonic. The buildings, besides the two above-mentioned churches and probably a few other buildings within the prince's seat (the chapel and the tower), were made of wood.

This was the city that Prince Mściwoj II, threatened by the Brandenburg dynasty, on the one hand, and by the Teutonic Knights, on the other, gave, together with the whole of Gdańsk Pomerania, to Prince Przemysł II. Przemysł became the ruler of this land after Mściwoj's death in 1294 but was murdered in Rogoźno just over a year later. Disputes over Gdańsk Pomerania after his death only ended when Władysław the Short came to power in Gdańsk in 1306.

In the face of a new invasion by the Brandenburg margraves, the commander of the Polish defenders of the town summoned the Teutonic Knights, who were then liege men of the Polish king, to their aid. The Teutonic Knights came to their help but, later, conquered the town by treachery. On November 13th, 1308, they attacked it, burnt it and killed a number of inhabitants. Excavations confirm this, for the layer dating back to the beginning of the 14th century shows distinct traces of a fire. It was thus by deceit and crime that Gdańsk came under the Teutonic Order's rule and, although the papal courts twice ordered the Knights to return the pillaged lands, the Order had no intention of giving way.

WITHIN MEDIEVAL WALLS

After the Teutonic Knights conquered Gdańsk, they first settled in the part of town that had not been destroyed, possibly in the Prince's former seat and then began to build a stone castle. They obviously considered the place where the castle-town had been built there hundred years earlier well chosen, as they built their castle in the same spot, the only difference being that it was more regular in shape. The castle port was also kept in the same place, but the western branch of the Motława was converted into a moat. Since the castle was later destroyed completely we can only guess what it looked like then. The High Castle, probably rectangular in shape, possibly took up the eastern part of the grounds. In the west and north, and perhaps partly in the south, the Low Castle, containing ancillary and farm buildings, adjoined it. The construction of such an imposing building, especially on marshy soil, would necessarily take many years. The basic work was finished, one can assume, in the 1340's.

The first settlement within Gdańsk to be mentioned during the rule of the Teutonic Knights was Osiek (Hachilwerk). This included the area to the west of the castle moat and east of St Catherine's Church. In the south it was bounded by the main approach to the castle (now Podwale Staromiejskie Street). Already in 1312, the Teutonic Knights had confirmed the inhabitants of Osiek in their former privileges. This, when taken together with the fact that Osiek was partly located on the site of the former Slavonic *suburbium*, seems to suggest that the Slavonic population was permitted or even ordered to live there. They were presumably local inhabitants who had survived the slaughter or people brought from outside to help with construction and other work. No information has been passed down about the building of Osiek; it is known, however, that it remained independent and maintained some form of self-rule during the entire rule of the Teutonic Knights.

In the area to the south of the Church of St Nicholas where a new settlement was built, probably as early as the 13th century, there existed in the 1330's, according to the oldest land-registers, rows of buildings along the present streets of Ogarna, Długi Targ, Piwna, Chlebnicka and Świętego Ducha.

The construction of the defence walls of the Main Town was started in 1343 with the Corner Tower. Like other towers of that period, it was open from the side of the city; the various tiers were divided by wooden ceilings, non-existent today

Quite different forms were given to another tower called Jacek, which probably also dated from the 14th century

Not until 1343 did this complete settlement, known as Główne Miasto (Main Town), receive its municipal charter. It seems therefore that the Teutonic Knights were not its founders. On the contrary, by failing to grant the city its charter until 35 years after they had conquered Gdańsk, they were, no doubt, trying to hamper its development until they had strengthened their position in this area.

A few years later, the former Dominican lands, between the streets of Szeroka and Podwale Staromiejskie, were added to the Main Town. Thus, the Main Town obtained the shape which it has preserved to the present day. It is a trapezium, measuring 550 metres and 550 to 850 metres, with its longest side along the Motława River.

The plan of this part of the city is unusual —

almost all the wider streets were built at right angles to the river and, the absence of a market place, so typical of Medieval cities, is striking. This particular street plan was due to the fact that Gdańsk was a port town. The quays played the role of a market place and the streets leading to them were used for transporting goods to the merchants' cellars and warehouses. In fact, out of 16 city gates, as many as 9 were built on the side by the river and only 7 on the remaining three sides. The basically regular plan of the Main Town, however, shows some irregularities in the lines of the streets, which is a result of the fact that some houses were already standing before the plan of the city was decided upon. The suggestion put forward by German scholars that the irregularities of the plan were due to the swampy subsoil appears unfounded, as the north-eastern part of the city, built in the second half of the 14th and in the 15th century on very swampy soil, is as regular as a chessboard.

The building of the defence walls of the Main Town began in 1343 and was continued for a century and a half, but the main work was completed in 1410. On the three "landward" sides, the city was surrounded by a wall which was even double in the south and west. At least nine gates were also built (the gates on the river were put up later) as well as over twenty towers of various kinds. On the landward side, the city was surrounded by a moat across which drawbridges led to the various gates.

The dwelling houses in the Main Town had timber frames filled in with plaster or brick. Not until the end of the 14th century were the houses constructed entirely of brick. The plan according to which the houses were built was adapted to the narrow and, mainly, rather deep building plots. The houses had three, sometimes only two, windows but they reached back 15, 20 and more metres and were two or even three storeys high.

The biggest building in the Main Town then was St Mary's Church, although it differed to a large extent both in shape and size from the present

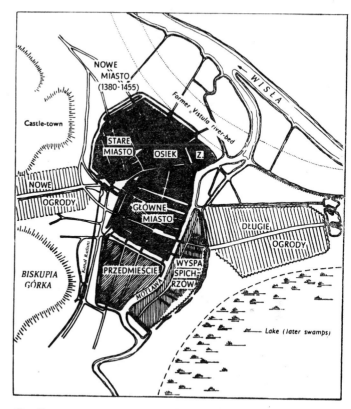

By the end of the 14th century the Medieval town complex was already formed. It included the Main Town, Old Town, Osiek, Castle (Z), Suburb, New Town, Granaries' areas (later Granary Island) and the suburban Long Gardens and New Gardens.

building. At that time it was a basilica (a higher nave and lower aisles) which now forms the western part of the present church, although the tower was lower. The building was converted into a typical Late Gothic "hall" church with the nave and three aisles of equal height in the early 15th century. The buildings put up in the 14th century — St John's Church, the Town Hall and the original Artus Court, the seat of the municipal guild — differed greatly from the present buildings. Only the Church of St Nicholas had already acquired its present shape. The extensive Dominican monastery buildings adjoined the church on its north side.

The city port already included the whole section of the Motława nearest to the Main Town. The merchants stored some of the goods in their homes or outbuildings, but as early as the 14th century warehouses and specially granaries were put up, mainly on the opposite, right side of the river. After the first line of buildings was put up, with an adjoining street (now called Chmielna), further building

The most strongly fortified was the western part of the Main Town, which was most exposed to danger. In that part, the most strongly built-up was the foregate in Długa Street serving as a barbican. Reconstruction of the foregate as it appeared at the end of the 15th century, according to Dr Ryszard Massalski

took place. In this way, a separate complex of granaries was set up — the later Granary Island.

The shipwrights' yards were located to the south of the Main Town, on the Motława River. Further on, to the west, a new suburb grew up, today known as Stare Przedmieście (Old Suburb). It owed its existence to the rapid development of the Main Town and the lack of space within its boundaries. Most of the buildings along the four streets parallel to the river were completed before 1400 and the construction begun of the Church of SS. Peter and Paul. The suburb was formally subordinate to the Main Town. Although the area was closely built up, houses were still wooden or half-timbered and, instead of defence walls, rather primitive earth fieldworks were built on the southern and western sides. To the north of the Main Town and west of Osiek was the part of the city which in the early 14th century was already known as Stare Miasto (Old Town). This proves that it must have existed before the year 1308, either as part of the Slavonic castle-town or as a separate settlement. During the first half of the 14th century the Old Town included the following streets: Garncarska, Elżbietańska, Kowalska, Korzenna and Rajska, together with the Church of St Catherine; later on this section was extended to the east. Then a new street, Łagiewniki, was built and its extension Stolarska Street was laid out on territory taken over from Osiek. In the 1360's the Old Town already had some form of self-government and, around 1380, a Town Hall was built on Korzenna Street, which may be considered proof of the fact that a municipal charter was either granted or regained.

During the first half of the 14th century, a canal was built which brought the water of the Radunia River from Pruszcz, 11 kilometres away. The canal was led through the Old Town, perhaps along the route of some former sewer or canal. Many manufacturing enterprises, powered by water, were built over the canal and its numerous branches. These included mills, smithies, a tannery, a fulling-press and a sawmill. The most imposing of them all was

Dominican St Nicholas Church, dating back to the 13th century, acquired its present shape at the beginning of the 15th century

the Big Mill built on an island. It had mill-wheels on each side and as many as six storeys of granaries under a huge roof above the hand-mills set up on two tiers.

At the turn of the 14th century, the church and cloister of St Bridget and the church and hospital of St Elizabeth were built in the Old Town. All these buildings later underwent alterations. The residential buildings were first wooden or half-tim-

bered, and brick buildings were put up much later than in the Main Town.

At that time, the Old Town did not have defence walls; it was probably protected from the west by an earth dike and from the north by a primitive moat. In the north-east, on the Vistula, there were probably no defences.

In 1380 the Grand Master of the Teutonic Order issued settlement rights to Młode Miasto (Young

The largest industrial structure of Medieval Gdańsk: the Big Mill on the Radunia Canal, according to a drawing by Karol Steinbrecht from 1880

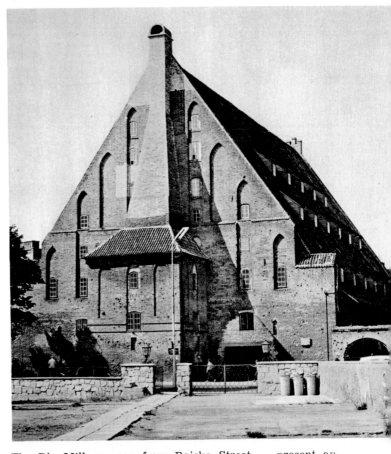

The Big Mill as seen from Rajska Street — present appearance. At the gable end, an old baking oven

Town). This town was to be much larger than the Main Town. It was to be located to the north of the Old Town between the Vistula and the edge of the upland. We know almost nothing about the way it was planned and built and, frankly, it is one of the mysteries of Gdańsk. Theoretically, this town which lay right on the Vistula, near its mouth and, at least partly on ground which it was easy to build on, had excellent prospects and might have been expected to rival the remaining Gdańsk communities, especially the Main Town. However, its development could not have been very rapid, and it

probably did not reach the expected dimensions, since it was pulled down in the second half of the 15th century.

Still other, more village-like suburbs belonged to the municipal complex of Medieval Gdańsk. Long gardens were built to the east of the granaries on low-lying land which was almost a depression, on the road leading to Żuławy. Apart from gardens, this area included ropemakers' workshops and residential building near today's Szopa Street. During the first half of the 15th century St Barbara's Church was built on Elbląska Street. In the Siedlecka Valley, to the west of the city, on the road to Chmielno, the settlement of New Gardens grew up (the present Świerczewskiego Street). Further away, many villages arose, such as Orunia, Siedlce, Wrzeszcz and Zaroślak at the foot of Biskupia Górka which today form part of the city of Gdańsk. In the second half of the 14th century, the church

St James' Church built in the Old Town in the 15th century was a seamen's church. The Baroque spire was transferred in the second half of the 19th century from the torn-down St James' Gate

The Cistercian Church at Oliwa, built in the style of a high basilica, was extended in the second half of the 14th century. Present view from the side of the chancel

and Cistercian monastery were rebuilt and extended after a fire. They then largely received their present shape except that there was no vault in the main nave or transept and that some of the monastery buildings were put up later.

Slowly, imperceptibly on the whole but sometimes violently, changes occurred in the city as in its surrounding. The forests, which used to cover almost the whole upland and the drier parts of Żuławy, were cut down for building, for piles and the

Sections of the walls of the Teutonic castle have been preserved in the walls of houses at 8 and 9 Wartka Street (in the photo: 9 Wartka Street)

The towers erected in the second half of the 15th century had rounded shapes. One of the suburb's towers — Pod Zrębem (Frame) Tower

construction of quays and, finally, for shipbuilding and even for export. In Żuławy, as the river continued to deposit silt, pools became overgrown and drainage schemes were undertaken. The volume of water diminished, and there was increasingly more arable land and meadows. Among other changes the great lake formed by the flood waters of the Vis-

tula to the east and south-east of the complex of Medieval settlements, on the site of the present suburbs of Olszynka and Błonie, began to disappear. At the same time, the Vistula made a sudden change in its course, several hundred metres to the north of the castle. This must have happened during one of the great floods, perhaps in 1371. The former

The coat of arms of the city and that of Royal Prussia, with the Polish eagle between them, was an emblem frequently seen in Gdańsk. The preserved coats of arms on the reconstructed Straganiarska (Standkeepers') Gate

river bed became a gradually disappearing backwater; the city gained new ground of which the land lying towards the north-east of the castle was the first to be occupied by shipwrights.

At the beginning of the 15th century, the inhabitants of Gdańsk were estimated at about 20,000, of whom 15,000 probably lived in the Main Town. There were great changes in the balance of the population caused by the large-scale immigration of German settlers, especially among merchants and the more prosperous classes. Even so, relations with the Teutonic Order were not too happy. In the

The Crane — a mighty defence structure and, at the same time, a harbour crane, was used for the reloading of heavy objects and for putting up masts on ships

second half of the 14th century, riots broke out twice and were cruelly suppressed by the Order. After the defeat of the Teutonic Knights at Grunwald, in 1410, the townsmen hurried to pay homage to King Władysław Jagiełło. The Teutonic Knights took revenge and secretly assassinated the mayors of the Main Town — Leczkow and Hecht, as well as one of the councillors. This, of course, brought increased hatred, which was also caused by economic factors, especially the high duties. All this

taken together, induced Gdańsk to join the cities which formed the Prussian Union in 1440. The secret aim of the Union was to liberate Pomerania from the Teutonic yoke.

On February 4th, 1454, the Prussian Union renounced its allegiance to the Teutonic Order and, the next day the citizens of Gdańsk took up arms against its local representatives, who were forced to withdraw. After 145 years of the Order's rule, Gdańsk returned to Poland and committed itself to the protection of King Casimir the Jagiellon, who confirmed the city's accession to Poland by an act of incorporation issued in March of the same year. The beginnings were not easy — the Order had no intention of giving in and the Thirteen Years' War was unleashed. During this the Teutonic troops plundered the neighbourhood of Gdańsk. The forces and fleet formed by the citizens of Gdańsk aided the Polish army, and also took part in the capture of Malbork. Large financial contributions collected by the inhabitants of Gdańsk and presented to the king, also helped to win the final victory.

One of the first steps that the inhabitants of Gdańsk took within their city was to demolish the castle of the Teutonic Knights, or to be more exact, its main part, the High Castle. The building material gained from the demolition of the castle was used for building a number of houses, especially in the suburban area. At the beginning of 1445, after they had received the king's consent, the townsmen began to demolish the competitive Young Town which obviously was a thorn in their side. Its inhabitants had to move to the remaining parts of Gdańsk and the houses were pulled down. The parish church and monastery, which were left at first, were later also dismantled and completely rebuilt within the Old Town. Only the southern part remained, together with the Church of St James which was built in the first half of the 15th century and included in the Old Town.

In recognition of the fidelity of the inhabitants of Gdańsk and their great contribution, especially financial, to the Thirteen Years' War, Casimir the

Late Gothic houses received rich moulding and finials. Façade of the house at 75/76 Szeroka Street, carefully restored in 1966

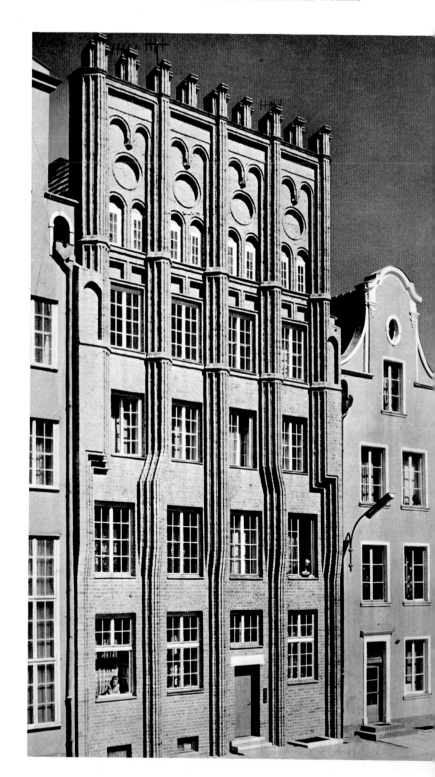

Jagiellon rewarded the city in a truly royal manner, by granting it, in the years 1454—1477, six charters one after another. The most important of them, the so-called "great privilege," was issued in Gdańsk on May 15th, 1457, and bestowed important economic and autonomous rights on the town. Especially important was the fact that the city was allowed the right to decide about the opening and closing of the port; however, the king or his representative in Gdańsk, or one of the town councillors had to agree each time. The city also gained the right to decide about settlement permits for foreign merchants which, as a result, left the monopoly of trade in the hands of Gdańsk merchants. This became the basis of the townsmen's prosperity. In the next privilege, issued ten days later, on May 25th, 1457, also in Gdańsk, Casimir the Jagiellon bestowed honorary rights on the town. The royal crown, placed above the two crosses that were formerly the town's coat of arms was considered proof of special royal favour.

The "great privilege" of May 15th, 1457, was also of great importance to the expansion of the city. It abolished the divisions of the Gdańsk communities and set up an overall local authority. And although the Old Town still tried to keep its autonomy, motivated by either ambitions or by resentment against the hegemony of the Main Town, the basis was created for the formation of a uniform municipal body.

One of the earliest signs that the city was becoming united, and an important factor in making further consolidation possible, was the common defensive system surrounding the whole city. The building of this system was begun in the localities that, up till then, had been least fortified, that is, the Old Town and Suburb, which were surrounded

29

In the second half of the 15th century, St Mary's Church was extended and received its present form. Traces of changes in the original concept can be seen in walls running into windows — as in the corner of the south aisle and the transept

Three aisles of equal height and rows of side chapels, only slightly lower than the aisles, form the huge, hall-like interior of St Mary's Church

by defence walls in the second half of the 15th century. Five gates were built within these walls: three in the part around the Old Town and two in that around the Suburb. The towers and gates differed from the former fortifications in being round in shape. The earthworks of the Old Town and Suburb were connected with the walls of the Main Town which also supplemented its fortifications by building a few new towers and the rest of the gates on the Motława, and at the same time, incorporating the walls of the castle which had belonged to the Teutonic Knights in the system. The Crane, a defence building which was a gate and also a powerful crane that would lift weights of as much as two tons to a height of 30 metres, was used to load heavy objects and putting up masts on ships, also received its final shape during that time.

Building these walls resulted in a certain expansion of the city towards the north and north-east; it also settled the boundaries of the Old Town and Suburb. Building the gates resulted in the increased or decreased importance of some streets, for example, the route from Elżbietańska to Garncarska Street lost much of its significance. At the same time, the former crossroads turned into the Timber Market.

In residential building, no important changes occurred. However, brick houses were built more often, especially in the Main Town. They already reached five storeys in height and their appearance was more varied with pointed Gothic recesses and more elaborate gables. Terraces projecting from the house quite high above street level and hiding the entrance to the cellar also began to appear. High, sculptured stone slabs were set up at the stairs leading to these terraces. This was the prototype of the terraces which later became so characteristic of Gdańsk.

In church architecture, the division of the city into six parishes and the desire to build high tow-

Lace-like gables crown the Late Gothic Holy Trinity Church and St Anne's Chapel

Contrasting with the splendour of the gables is the austere simplicity of the interior of the Franciscan Holy Trinity Church

ers, which previously was opposed by the Teutonic Knights, resulted in great activity. At that time, additions were made to almost all the Gdańsk churches. They were often made higher and changed into "hall" churches. The system of internal buttresses is typical of the Gdańsk churches. These allowed for additional rows of side chapels, while the outer walls retained their unbroken line. Extending St Mary's Church was the most important work undertaken; the side naves were widened and made higher in the older, western part, and the church was given its present hall shape. At the same time, the tower was built up to the present height. In 1502, this largest church in Poland was completed

The northern, Gothic, wall of Artus Court. The upper part rebuilt after war destruction

The Late Gothic Court of the St George Fraternity of Marksmen, erected in the area inside the wall, near the gate closing Długa Street

after 160 years by the addition of an unusual vaulted ceiling.

Of the newly built church buildings which were put up in that time, it is worth mentioning St Bartholomew's Church, the Carmelite monastery which was finished only in part, St Joseph's Church in the Old Town (transferred from the New Town) and, in the Suburb — the Holy Trinity Church with St Anne's Chapel, a beautiful example of Late Gothic, which was begun te the beginning of the 15th century but not completed until the 1520's.

The tower of the Main Town Hall was built during the second half of the 15th century and the eastern wall was finished with an attic and turrets. Here, as in many other buildings which were put up or rebuilt during that time, there is a noticeable influence of Flemish architecture. At about the same time, a new Artus Court was built in place of the old one, which had been burnt down; its magnificent hall was spanned by a star-vault ceiling supported by four slim, granite columns. In the years 1487—1494 the patrician St George's Society of Marksmen built itself a new seat between the walls, to the north of the gate on Długa Street.

At the beginning of the 16th century, the former ditch or swampy old backwater dividing the granaries area from the east was turned into a moat. Probably at the same time, the so-called "dog's dike" was built in the east and south, to better secure the island that was formed by the new moat. The uninhabited area of Granary Island was closed and guarded by dogs at night, to secure it against thieves and fire started through negligence — hence the name of the dike. This name disappeared, together with the dike, but the street along which the dogs were led to the island is still called Ogarna (Hound) Street.

A part of the western façade of the Court of the St George Fraternity reveals the austere beauty of Gothic brick architecture

A new gate — Stągiewna (Milk-can) was built in the years 1517—1519 on the road leading to the Long Gardens, in line with the "dog's dike." It consists of two towers and differs greatly from those built previously. The larger, circular tower did not have a roof in its original form but was topped by a platform for guns supported by strong vaulting. For a new period had begun, the age of science and technology and of great geographical discoveries. Apart from discoveries and improvements that served peacetime interests, the technique of war was also improved. The improvement of artillery proved to have the most far-reaching effects, since it now became a really dangerous weapon, able even to destroy walls. This was noted quite early in Gdańsk and that is why, in the years 1515—1520, the western part of the walls of the Old Town and the Suburb which were the most endangered, was reinforced by the powerful earthen ramparts. Medieval walls had entered upon their decline.

The Stągwie (Milk-can) towers guarding the granary area from the east were the last Medieval fortification in Gdańsk

PERIOD OF SPLENDOUR

The 16th and 17th centuries brought little peace to Poland. Although the war with the Teutonic Knights ended by the secularization of the Order and Homage paid to Sigismund the Old, the many wars with the Duchy of Muscovy and the Russian state which then was being set up, fights with the Swedes over Livonia, Swedish invasions caused by dynastic conflicts, Cossack uprisings, and wars with Turkey — all these events exhausted the country, undermined its economy and brought about the decline of its cities. In spite of these unfavourable circumstances, Gdańsk reached the zenith of its prosperity precisely at that time.

The city's return to Poland in 1454, the recovery of its whole natural hinterland, the assurance of a monopoly position in the handling of Polish overseas trade and the numerous privileges granted by the Polish kings, all created a basis not only for the town's economic development but even for its wealth. The inhabitants of Gdańsk understood this well. In defending their many privileges, they even went so far as to resort to armed conflict over the king's privateers, during the reign of Sigismund Augustus and armed resistance during the reign of Stefan Batory. However, in difficult times, the people always proved their allegiance to Poland, and Gdańsk deserved the description of "a town loyal to the Republic." This was distinctly noticeable especially during the wars with Sweden: the first time was in the years 1626—1627, when the environs of the city were plundered and the blockage of the Gdańsk port, which lasted for many months, was finally ended with the victory of the Polish fleet at Oliwa, and the second time was during the Swedish deluge which flooded the whole country, when Gdańsk remained one of the very few Polish cities not taken by the enemy.

This period of economic development coincided with the great cultural and ideological revolution of the Renaissance. The Reformation and the development of philosophy brought by it, new discoveries, the development of technology, new trends in literature, painting and sculpture, new styles in architecture — all this found receptive ground and rich patrons in Gdańsk. Architects who were living in the town or were specially invited, sculptors and

Allegorical drawing from the Gdańsk astronomer Hevelius' work *Uranographia*, published in Gdańsk in 1687. In the lower right, a panorama of Gdańsk

painters created works of art of which the city was proud and which often gained international fame. Among those active at this time in Gdańsk there were especially many Flemish and Dutch builders and artists. Anthonis van Opberghen, Wilhelm, Abraham and Izaak van den Blocke, Hans Vredemann de Vries, Paul van Dorne, Frederic Hendrikson Vroom, Cornelius van dem Bosch, Jan Wijbe, Wilhelm van den Meer and others. Of course there were also Germans: Johann Kramer, Anton Möller, Bartholomäus Ranisch, Andreas Schlüter and Daniel

Schultz. There were also Poles — of whom, first of all, Jan and Jerzy Strakowski, and Jeremiasz Falck, who signed himself Polonus, deserve mention.

Not only architecture but painting and sculpture also flourished. There were many outstanding cabinet and clock makers, goldsmiths, bell-founders and medallists, craftsmen producing amber goods and wrought iron work, wood carvers and masons. The products of Gdańsk craftsmen adorned both public buildings and homes of the burghers and were widely exported.

The rich Gdańsk burghers supported the development of art and learning and were often no mean scholars. Among the many, we should mention the poet, humanist and diplomat and, at the same time, royal counsellor, Jan Dantyszek (1485—1548) and the astronomer Jan Hevelius (1611—1687), author of scientific works, constructor of astronomic instruments (including a huge telescope) and discoverer of a constellation which he named Sobieski's Shield. The renowned physicist, Gabriel Fahrenheit (1686—1736), was also a native of Gdańsk. The historical, biological and medical sciences also flourished. It is worth pointing out that a small hospital ward was founded in the 1620's, the first on Polish soil. The setting up of a high school — the Academic College — in the second half of the 16th century also encouraged the development of learning. It was proud of its high standards which were almost up to university level. In the school building (a former Franciscan monastery) the Municipal Library was founded with an excellent collection of books. Apart from this, there existed many large private book collections in the town. In order to complete this picture, one should also mention the printing houses active in Gdańsk from the beginning of the 16th century, which printed various works including scientific dissertations. A large proportion were published in Polish and, what is significant, approximately 90 various manuals for learning Polish were also published. Polish was the native tongue of the poorer city inhabitants and of those who lived in the city's environs. The wealthy, mostly merchants who had come here from other countries, learned Polish from the manuals and at special classes held at the Academic College, so that the use of the language became more and more common.

Since increasing riches were being accumulated within the city, its inhabitants had good reason to fear enemy conquest. However, the city could afford the great expense of improving its defensive installations. So it is not at all surprising that the fortifications were subject to special care and were almost constantly being rebuilt and modernized.

Jan Łaganowski (pen-name: Stephani) was a teacher of the Polish language in the Academic College in Gdańsk in 1678—1690. He also ran a special Polish school; its inauguration was announced by this bilingual notice

The Panorama of Gdańsk from the west, made by Jakub Hoffman in 1630, dedicated to Chamberlain Adam Kazanowski, shows the city already protected by earthen ramparts

In the 1530's, the western walls were replaced by earth-works, which were more resistant to artillery bombardment. In front of the line of ramparts three large earth structures called roundels were put up in the moat; the first one was circular in shape but the next two were really proper towers. The first regular tower was built in 1571—1575 and modelled on Italian fortifications which were then the most advanced. This was the Karowy Tower, located at the entrance to Podwale Przedmiejskie Street, now called Leningradzka Avenue. Both this and three further towers built to the south had high escarps and casemates and on their west side were protected by a wide moat. In the western part of the rampart, on the axis of Długa Street, Wyżynna (Upland) Gate was built in the years 1574—1575 but not until 1588 was it given its stone Renaissance finish. The building that has been preserved to the

This is what Upland Gate looked like in the times when it was part of the city's defences. Access to the city was protected by an escarped rampart and a wide fosse with a draw-bridge over it. Lithograph from 1832, by Meyerheim

Upland Gate was given a rich stone decoration. Section of the frieze of the west elevation from 1588

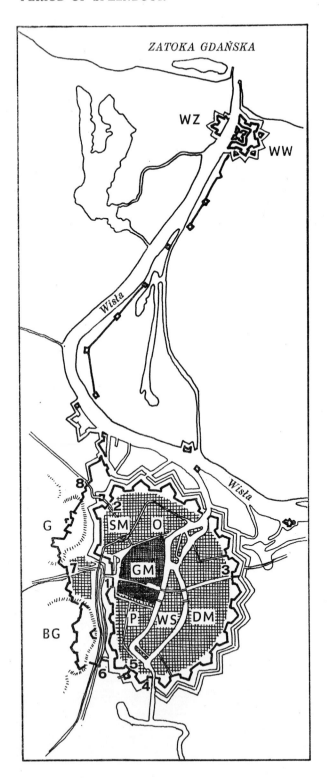

ZATOKA GDAŃSKA

present day is only part of the gate-house. (The other part, together with two passages set at an angle, was on the edge of the former foregate of Długa Street, and the traffic went through both of its sides.) At about the same time the foregate was adapted for use as a prison. Beautiful Renaissance gables were added to the Torture Chamber and a spire to the Prison Tower.

The building of the powerful ring of fortifications around the city was not undertaken until the years 1620—1635, according to a design by Cornelius van dem Bosch, when fourteen towers of the Dutch type without casemates were built. They were surrounded by a moat and encircled the town on the south, east and north sides. Three gates were built within the line of the fortifications: Żuławska, Nizinna (Lowland) and St James (the first two have been preserved to the present day). The Stone Sluice was a much more difficult problem for the engineers; it was built at the mouth of the Motława which had shifted eastward. It made possible not only the regulation of the water level in the river and moats but also the flooding, if necessary, of the low-lying areas which surrounded the town in the east and south. Other hydro-engineering enterprises were connected with the building of earth fortifications. The Radunia Canal was led into the city by an aqueduct over the moat and a special culvert under the rampart. To avoid a second crossing the then

Renaissance and Baroque fortifications embraced the town with a strong ring reinforced from the western side by an additional line which included Grodzisko and Biskupia Górka. A chain of reinforcements along the Vistula linked the town with Wisłoujście Fortress.

GM — Główne Miasto (Main Town), SM — Stare Miasto (Old Town), O — Osiek, P — Przedmieście (Suburb), WS — Wyspa Spichrzów (Granary Island), DM — Dolne Miasto (Lower City), BG — Biskupia Górka, G — Grodzisko, WW — Wisłoujście, eastern rampart, WZ — Wisłoujście, western rampart.

1. Upland Gate 2. St James' Gate 3. Żuławy Gate 4. Stone Sluice 5. Lowland Gate 6. Orunia Gate 7. Siedlce Gate 8. Oliwska Gate

Żuławy Gate designed by Jan Strakowski closed the eastern entrance to the city — Elbląska Street. At one time, it also had a fosse and a drawbridge like the Upland Gate

Lowland Gate — one of the three existing Renaissance gates, and the only one to preserve its former surroundings: the ramparts and fosse

A part of the Stone Sluice. In the background on the right — a part of the Żubr (Bison) Rampart

The Wisłoujście Fortress. The photo shows the beacon tower rebuilt from war destruction, the brick "wreath" surrounding it, and the north-western part of the fortress — Artillery Bastion

existing mouth of the Vistula was filled in and the canal was directed to the east, to the Motława, along the line of Medieval moats.

The Radunia Canal was also used in the 16th century for improving the Gdańsk water conduits. Although Gdańsk already had piped water in the 14th century, this was only a system of wooden pipes which by gravitation brought the water from the Siedlecki Stream to wells within the city. In the 1530's a special pump was built, which was rebuilt after being destroyed in 1577; it was powered by the waters of the Radunia Canal and forced the water into the city's conduits.

Since artillery now had greater range the city was in danger from two hills: Grodzisko and Biskupia Górka. For that reason, the first fieldwork on Biskupia Górka was built in the 1630's and at the same time the towers of the western line, which had been built earlier, were improved. It is interesting to note that during this work the Dutchman Jan Wijbe used a cable car by which earth was transported from Biskupia Górka. In the middle of the 17th century, during the second Swedish invasion, an additional line of fortifications was built; they protected the city in the west and included both Biskupia Górka and Grodzisko. In the north, these fortifications led to the Vistula and, in the south, they were connected with the defence ring surrounding the city. In these additional, western fortifications, three gates were built: Oliwska, Siedlecka and Oruńska. Of one of these the name only — Oliwska Gate — has survived; the two others, on the other hand, have disappeared without any trace at all.

Apart from the city itself, the mouth of the Vistula was of special strategic importance to Gdańsk. Probably in the middle of the 15th century, a watch-

In the years 1559-1560, Daniel Dirksen erected on the tower of the Main Town Hall a slender Renaissance spire with a statue of King Sigismund Augustus on top of it

The monumental Gothic eastern façade of the Main Town Hall was crowned in the second half of the 16th century with a fine Early Renaissance stone attic

The new fortifications caused changes in the city plan. In the western part of the Old Town where the existing buildings came closest to the hills, it became necessary to abandon a number of plots and even houses. This was also the case in the Long Gardens area where strategical considerations (the line of fortifications was not extended) required that the former suburb be divided into two, and part of it left beyond the line of reinforcements. This was repeated 20 years later, when the exterior western continuation was being built, within the area of New Gardens. But the city did not only have territorial losses, for new land was also surrounded by the ring of towers and included in its area. The largest such plot lay to the south of Long Gardens; swampy and intersected by drainage ditches, nothing was built on it for a long time. Some grounds

The most magnificent room in the interior of the Main Town Hall, rebuilt in Renaissance style, was the Summer Council Room, also called the Red Hall, modelled after Venetian interiors and equalling them in the wealth of decoration

tower already existed there. In 1482 it was replaced by a brick tower which at the same time served as a lighthouse (it stood almost on the edge of the sea which was very gradually receding.) At the beginning of the 16th century, additional reinforcements were built near the tower; in 1562, it was surrounded by a round, brick fort known as a "wreath". At the turn of the 16th century a fort with four towers was built around the "wreath" and in the years 1624—1626 it was encircled by an earth rampart with five towers. This is how the Wisłoujście Fortress was set up and, although its exterior was rebuilt and changed many times, its care has remained to the present day and is a beautiful and rare example of a port fortress. To assure communication with Wisłoujście and to make navigation on the Vistula partially secure, a chain of reinforcements was built between the mouth and the city in the years 1638—1658.

The Renaissance Town Hall was erected in the years 1587—1595 by Anthonis van Opberghen, on the site of the former Gothic Town Hall

were also gained to the north-east from the Old Town and south of Granary Island. A belt of land, narrow but important to the city, was gained by filling in some of the Medieval moats at the western outskirts of the Main Town. The Coal Market was set up on this and, to the south of it, a street, today called Bogusławskiego.

Although the reinforcements of the Main Town were completely inside the fortifications, by then, and had lost their military significance, they were still kept up and were even further maintained (only the moats were destroyed). Most probably, the richest of the burghers who lived in the Main Town considered the walls and gates a protection against the occasional demonstrations of the common people who lived in the other parts of the city. According to historical sources, riots took place a few times and, twice, Polish kings even had to play the role of mediator. As a result of the increasing social processes and of the mediation of Sigismund the Old, the municipal government changed and the Third Order was added to the Council and Bench, to represent the interests of the artisans and all the poorer people. After a century and a half, it turned out that the Third Order, taken over by the patrician class, did not perform its real role and the poorer classes again searched for help, at the court of Polish King John Sobieski, who assured them a real part in the government of the city by special decree.

The Renaissance style in architecture, that originated in Italy in the first half of the 15th century, appeared in the south of Poland at the beginning

Upper part of portal of the Old Town Hall. Above the entrance, between two angels — the Polish eagle

The Great Arsenal — the most magnificent work of Gdańsk Renaissance, built in the first years of the 17th century by Jan Strakowski, after Opberghen's design. Western façade as seen from the Coal Market

of the 16th century, but came to Gdańsk only in the second half of the century. The influence of Antwerp Mannerism with its use of florid ornament was especially strong in Gdańsk.

The first known Renaissance building in Gdańsk was the orphanage at St Elizabeth's Hospital. This house was later demolished but the stone portal and ornamental gable were placed on the southern façade of the new building at 38 Wały Jagiellońskie Street.

In the years 1559—1560, the tower of the Main Town Hall was surmounted by a new Renaissance cupola and a statue of King Sigismund Augustus. At the same time, a carillon with many bells was installed in the tower. Somewhat later, a beautiful attic of stone tracery was added to the eastern wall of the Town Hall on which were displayed the coats of arms of Poland, Gdańsk and Royal Prussia. At the end of the 16th century, the space under the roof of the Town Hall was converted into a normal storey and, at the same time, part of the interior of the Town Hall was rebuilt in the Renaissance style. The richly decorated summer Council Room, known as the Red Hall, and modelled on Venetian interiors, was the most beautiful of the chambers.

Also towards the end of the century a Renaissance Town Hall with a slender spire was built in place of the former Gothic Town Hall of the Old Town.

In the years 1600—1609, the greatest and most splendid example of the Gdańsk Renaissance style was built — the Arsenal. This building, built by Jan Strakowski, according to a design by Anthonis van

A detail of the sculptural decoration of the Arsenal — part of the portal in the western façade

The southern façade of Artus Court was rebuilt twice, in the 16th and in the 17th century. The present form dates from the years 1616—1617, and was designed by Abraham van den Blocke

The portal of Artus Court was decorated with medallions — the left one representing King Sigismund III Vasa, the right one — Prince Władysław (later King Władysław IV)

Opberghen, stood in a line with the former walls of the Main Town, at the Coal Market and overlooked the eastern end of Piwna Street.

The main façade of Artus Court was also rebuilt in Renaissance style. The first changes were introduced in the first half of the 16th century but it received its present form in the years 1616—1617, when an attic and a new portal, decorated with medallions of King Sigismund III and Prince Władysław (the later Władysław IV), were added according to a design by Abraham van den Blocke. At

Golden Gate was erected on the site of the former Gothic gate of Długa Street. It was built by Abraham van den Blocke in the style of Italian Renaissance but with Manneristic, typically Dutch decorations

Green Gate which closes the Long Market from the side of the Motława, was rebuilt in Renaissance style by Jan Kramer from Dresden and Regnier from Amsterdam; hence, the visible mixture of Saxon and Dutch influence

that time, the interior of the Court also received most of its rich furnishings such as paneling, pictures, sculptures and an ornamental stove. In the 1630's, a beautiful fountain with a statue of the mythological ruler of the seas — Neptune — was set up in front of the building. The gates in the fence,

St Catherine's Church, one of Gdańsk's oldest, its beginnings dating back to the first half of the 13th century, received a fine spire in 1634 with forms dating from Renaissance to Baroque

In St Nichola's Church, a superb Late Renaissance high altar has been preserved

The façade of the house at 35 Długa Street was modelled after Italian architectural patterns. Because of the sculptured lions on the portals, it was called Lion's Castle

The stone façade of the house at 41 in the Long Market, called the Golden House, was adorned with fine sculptural decoration and rich gildings

which are fine examples of Gdańsk wrought iron work, were decorated with the coats of arms of Gdańsk and with Polish eagles.

All four gates in the fortifications were given Renaissance shapes — the most highly decorated Upland Gate, finished in 1588, as well as the Lowland, Żuławska and St James' gates that were built in the 1620's. Earlier, in the years 1564—1568, Zielona (Green) Gate, which stood at the eastern end of Długi Targ Street, was also rebuilt in Renaissance style. And in the years 1612—1614 Abraham van

den Blocke rebuilt the former Gothic gate (now the Golden Gate) at Długa Street and gave it its present form.

In sacral building, the influences of the Renaissance were evident much later and the style was much less widely represented, both due to the fact that many Medieval churches were still extant and also to the spreading Reformation. The towers of St Bartholomew's and Corpus Christi churches, which were built in the 1590's, were still Gothic in form. Late Renaissance form was given to the

Small-size bricks and stone decorative elements are the characteristic features of Dutch Renaissance; it was in this style that the Late Renaissance House of the Pelplin Abbots was built

Also shaped under distinct Dutch influence were the façades, and especially the portals with transom windows, of the Late Renaissance houses at 44 and 43 (formerly 54) Ogarna Street

tower of St Bridget's built at the beginning of the 17th century, and a beautiful Renaissance cupola as well as the second Gdańsk carillon were put on the tower of St Catherine's Church in 1634. The Renaissance style is much more apparent in church furnishings, such as altars, epitaphs, organs and pulpits and here it is often under the influence of Antwerp Mannerism.

The Renaissance burghers' mansions did not basically differ, in exterior or interior, from the Late Gothic houses. The incorporation of the staircase into the interior of the house, allowed, to a great degree, for the extension of the entrance hall, which was now richly decorated and became a reception room. Important changes took place in the outside appearance of the houses. In Gdańsk there were two types of façades: brick, with florid stone ornamentation (the Dutch type); and frontal elevations of several orders of pilasters. Stone houses modelled on Italian architecture were exceptional. The most splendid façade of this type is to be found in the burgher's house known as Golden on Długi Targ Street. The Renaissance terraces, most often, had decorative balustrades.

The period when the Baroque style appeared in Gdańsk is difficult to specify because the city shows transitional forms. One of the first Baroque buildings was the Small Arsenal built by Jerzy Stra-

Characteristic for the burgher's houses in Gdańsk are the ornate entrance terraces. The terrace of the house at 5/6 in the Long Market (Formerly 29 Długa Street)

The largest and the most richly decorated part of the interior of a Gdańsk Renaissance house was the hallway. The arcaded wall of such a hallway from the house at 45 Długa Street, transferred during the reconstruction to the Old Town Hall, now graces its first floor interior

kowski in the Suburb in the years 1643—1645. In Gdańsk itself, the Baroque style is represented by fewer examples and those that do exist are usually relatively uninteresting. This is due to the fact that the country was exhausted by the long wars which could be felt even in Gdańsk. This is why the Baroque burghers' houses often had modest, smoothly plastered elevations and simple gables and the dec-

53

Richly decorated gables of the Baroque houses 9 and 10 in the Long Market

A part of the terrace of the house at 59 Piwna Street shows all the wealth of stone art

The Royal Chapel is one of the few Baroque sacral objects in Gdańsk. (Shown after reconstruction but before the renovation of the façade)

The spacious, richly decorated Baroque hallway of the house at 101 Świętego Ducha Street. Engraving by J. X. Schultz from 1857

In the city, which was crowded by the ring of fortifications, space was at a premium; however, during the Baroque period, green patches began to appear within its confines. These consisted mainly of trees, planted on the streets and casting shade

Town Council ordinance prohobiting any fire on ships near the granaries. issued in Polish on April 19th, 1730

orative elements were restricted to the portals and terraces which were now usually equipped with ordinary stone and occasionally balustrades. Of course, there did exist burghers' houses that had more richly ornamented gables and even whole façades.

However, the most beautiful monument of the Gdańsk Baroque is the Royal Chapel, of which King John III Sobieski was one of the founders. It was built in the years 1678—1681 by Bartholomäus Ranisch and Andreas Schlüter, perhaps according to sketches made by the famous architect Tilman van Gameren and was intended for the Gdańsk Catholics who had been deprived of St Mary's Church by the growing Evangelical community.

The gable of one of Gdańsk's finest Rococo houses at No. 29 in the Long Market

On the wall of the granary at 59 Chmielna Street, from the side of the Motława, the Baroque cartouche in stone has been preserved, with the name "Under the Crown", and the date: 1755

on the terraces and, in the suburban areas where there were fewer buildings, of small gardens adjoining the houses. The first public garden, called Labirynt or Błędnik, was laid out in 1708 in the northern part of the city, near the Oliwska Gate.

The Gdańsk port could not be confined within the area of the city any more even though the former moat, which enclosed Granary Island in the east, was deepened and changed into a port canal. The timber yards and places where corn was processed, that is, dried and cleaned, which required the most

room, were therefore transferred to the north of the city, to both banks of the Vistula; hence the present name Przeróbka which means processing. Here, it is worth noting that, exactly in the middle of the 17th century, the shipment of grain via Gdańsk reached the volume of 100,000 lasts, which is approximately 250,000 tons, annually, so that the city was one of the main grain ports in Europe.

In the second half of the 17th century, important changes occurred at the mouth of the Vistula through which the road from the sea to the Gdańsk

The stonework of Rococo terraces, intricately cut, was adorned with reliefs. The terrace stonework of the so-called Gdańsk Hallway (at No. 43 in the Long Market), restored after war destruction

The houses of poorer people had a much more modest appearance than those of the merchants. Here is a house with galleries, near Holy Trinity Church, also from the Baroque period

port led. For years, new ship channels had been searched for, marked and even dredged, among the shallows that grew increasingly more extensive, as the old passages were constantly obstructed by sediment. Therefore, the straits that formed between the land and the shallows near the western shore, were eagerly made use of. To protect them against obstruction by silt from the Vistula, a sluice was built in 1686 and, four years later, the first breakwater was built to protect the new entrance from

the sea. In 1717, the straits were changed into a regular canal. This is how the present Port Canal was built, except that it was then much narrower. Apart from the mouth of the Vistula, there now existed an entrance to the port, which was moved to the west almost two kilometres. In order to make navigation easier, a new lighthouse was built near it, and a more conveniently situated sluice was set up on the side of the Vistula. The shallows, located to the north of the Port Canal and to the west of the

57

Mateusz Deisch, Gdańsk engraver from the second half of the 18th century, depicted the characteristic types of artisans and street vendors. Their cries, noted down by Deisch, prove that the vendors were local Poles

mouth of the Vistula, grew constantly and in the end turned into an island. It was called West Plaate or Westerplatte.

In the 17th century, Gdańsk had approximately 77,000 inhabitants, a considerable population for those times. For comparison, it is worth noting that Cracow had then less than 20,000 inhabitants and Warsaw had only 23,000 even during the first half of the 18th century. However, a great plague attacked Gdańsk in 1709, which took 24,000 lives. As a result of this and other disasters, the number of inhabitants decreased to about 48,000. After this adversity others quickly followed. In 1734 King Stanisław Leszczyński, forced to leave Warsaw, took shelter in Gdańsk. The city sided with its legitimate ruler, not caring about the consequences. This re-

sulted in an almost five-month siege of the town by the Russian and Saxon armies which supported Augustus III. In order to save the town from complete destruction Leszczyński secretly fled to France.

Gdańsk paid dearly for its loyalty. About 1,800 buildings were destroyed or damaged and the suburbs were burnt. The burghers themselves flooded the surrounding areas for strategic reasons.

The political weakness and economic decline of Poland at that time did not create favourable conditions for reconstruction. It was not until more than ten years later that this acquired greater pace. The burghers' houses were reconstructed or completely rebuilt, in the Rococo, or later also Neo-Classical styles, and often both at once. In the interiors, which had the same layout as formerly, the entrance hall was changed — it was turned into a small office over which there was a decorated entresol and stairs were built by the opposite wall. Terraces were still built in front of the houses, but the stone slabs by the railings and posts at the entrances were decorated now in a different style. Although the economic situation of the city was difficult, in 1768 the Main Town Hall was given a new portal and a richly sculptured terrace. In the Long and New Gardens the foundations were laid for a number of palaces; among others, the Polish magnates, Karol Radziwiłł and the Mniszech family built residences for themselves.

Despite the unfavourable economic situation, intellectual life in Gdańsk developed. Outward evidence of this were the scientific societies, founded by the enlightened burghers, first of a literary character; they later also dealt with the natural sciences, Gotfryd Lengnich, a historian was one of the founders of the Literary Society. He was the teacher of Stanisław Augustus Poniatowski, later last king of Poland.

In the 16th and 17th centuries, in spite of fires and destruction during almost every war, the villages and suburban settlements developed. To the south of Zaroślak, Scottish craftsmen founded a settlement known as Stare Szkoty (Old Scots) at the beginning of the 16th century. In the early 17th century, the Jesuits built a church, a monastery and a college. The church was destroyed many times and was given its present shape in the middle of the 18th century.

The artisan settlement of Oruńskie Suburb, the neighbouring Stare Szkoty and, further towards the south, the villages of Orunia, Lipce and Święty Wojciech expanded, as did the agricultural village of Stogi, to the north-east of the city, and the fishing village of Brzeźno, to the west of the entrance to the port. Siedlce and Suchanin that bordered on Gdańsk in the west preserved their agricultural character. The village of Chełm, which belonged to the bishops of Włocławek expanded in the

The portal and terrace with which the Main Town Hall was adorned in 1778, had Neo-Classical forms already

A group of Neo-Classical houses at 62—66 Ogarna Street. The terrace at No. 65 is in Rococo style, the next to the right is a later one

12th century into a town inhabited mainly by artisans.

In the years 1768—1770, a great two-kilometre-long four-lane avenue lined by linden trees was laid out between Gdańsk and Wrzeszcz. Wrzeszcz was a village near which mills, sawmills and forges had been built on the Strzyża Stream from the 13th century onward. In the 17th century, more and more artisans began to settle here and some of them

founded the Nowe Szkoty (New Scots) settlement. The rich Gdańsk burghers began to build suburban residences in the neighbourhood. As many as eight such manor houses were built in Polanki, at the foot of the upland, between Wrzeszcz and Oliwa.

In Oliwa and the environs, the waters of the Oliwski Stream were used to power more than twenty manufacturing plants, some of which belonged to the monastery but most to the enterprising Gdańsk burghers. In 1577, the monastery and church of the Cistercians were plundered and burnt. These were rebuilt towards the end of the 16th century. Then the ceiling over the main nave and transept were completed and the interiors received rich Renaissance furnishings (the stalls, main altar, later transferred to the transept and also numerous epitaphia, tombstones and pictures). Two chapels were also built and the monastery refectory given its appearance. After the monastery church had been devastated during the Swedish wars, over

Also dating back from the middle of the 18th century is the Rococo palace and a part of the abbots' park at Oliwa modelled after French patterns

The big organ of the Cistercian Church in Oliwa — a superb musical instrument and, at the same time, a work of Rococo art of carving

twenty altars, among them the main altar, numerous portals and a pulpit were added in the Baroque style and most of them have survived to the present day. In 1660, events of great historical importance took place in the Oliwa abbey — Polish-Swedish negotiations were carried on here and, on May 3rd of the same year a peace treaty was signed.

During the time of Abbot Jacek Rybiński, in the middle of the 18th century, a Rococo palace was built and, next to it, a park was laid out based on a French design. The northern part of the park, in the style of English gardens, was laid out towards the end of the same century. In the late 18th century, the magnificent Rococo organs were also installed in the Oliwa abbey church. The monk, Jan Wulf, devoted 25 years of his life to building them

Houses built in the suburbs of Gdańsk bordering on the Żuławy were characteristic of that area where Mennonite settlers brought the influence of Dutch architecture. Arcaded house at 297 Jedności Robotniczej Street in Gdańsk-Lipce

PERIOD OF DEVELOPMENT AND DECLINE

In 1772 the first partition of Poland took place. Prussia captured Pomerania and Gdańsk; although, thanks to diplomatic measures, it was not fully taken over, it became an enclave on foreign territory. Oruńskie Suburb, Stare Szkoty, Chełm and Siedlce, and even worse — the shores of the Vistula and Westerplatte, together with the new entrance to the port, all these were now in the hands of the Prussians.

"That morning disaster fell onto my ill-fated home town like a vampire..." this is how an inhabitant of Gdańsk, Johanna Schopenhauer, mother of the great philosopher, felt and described these events in her diary. This is how other people who lived in Gdańsk felt, independently of their origin of the language they used.

The situation of the city became exceptionally difficult. The Prussian king, Frederick II, decided to force the town to surrender. High duties were imposed on and, at the entrance to the port, opposite Westerplatte, the building of a new port was begun and attempts were made at setting up a competitive town in the south-western suburbs. This was called Immediatstadt Stolzenberg and its centre was in Chełm. A full temporary blockade of the city was organized. In spite of this, after 21 years, when the Prussian army entered Gdańsk, during the second partition of Poland, they met with armed resistance. This impulsive action clearly illustrates the feelings of the inhabitants, though it could not stop the course of events: Gdańsk came under Prussian rule.

The inhabitants of Gdańsk responded to the abolition of self-government and former privileges granted to the city by resigning from municipal office, going into mourning, and even by emigration. The population fell to 36,000. "In the course of years we felt the burden of foreign violence more and more painfully and it had a more and more deleterious influence on the former welfare of my unhappy home town," wrote Johanna Schopenhauer. This judgment was undoubtedly right in respect to the prosperity of Gdańsk but, in comparison with the period between the first and second partitions, the economic situation of the city had somewhat improved: at the beginning of the 19th century the export of grain increased to approximately 120,000 tons. At that time Nowy Port began to develop, in spite of the fact that the main part of the port was still on the Motława. A settlement of the same name grew up next to it. To secure both the ports, the Prussian authorities built a few ramparts. The first road which connected Nowy Port with Gdańsk

Daniel Chodowiecki, painter and artist, coming from Gdańsk and working in Berlin, visited his native city in 1773. During that stay, he made numerous sketches representing well-known personalities. Shown here are Polish aristocrats: Countess Ledóchowska and Guardian of the Crown — Czacki

was Wiślna Street, which then reached Jana z Kolna Street.

At that time not much was being built in Gdańsk; it was more usual, as contemporaries testify, to find deserted houses. Of the public buildings, one should mention the Neo-Classical theatre built near the Coal Market in the years 1798—1801.

The echoes of the French Revolution that came to Gdańsk aroused hopes of independence, and the outbreak of the Franco-Prussian War fanned them. At the end of May 1807, after a siege that lasted twenty months, Gdańsk was taken by a French corps under Marshal Lefèbvre and Polish regiments commanded by General Giełgud. Unfortunately, the hopes of the inhabitants of Gdańsk, like those of the whole Polish nation, were not fulfilled. Napoleon had his own political aims. Instead of a united Poland, a truncated state, the Duchy of Warsaw was set up, while Gdańsk was turned into a Free City and was made into a military base. Because of this, the fortifications of Grodzisko and Biskupia Górka, Wisłoujście and Nowy Port were modernized and developed, and completely new fortifications were built, including Napoleon's Fort, over the present Kashubian Canal, and Dessaix's Fort, which defended the city from the east.

Although the city regained its former right of self-government, effects of both the British blockade and of the continental blockade, directed by Napoleon, lay heavily on its economy. The performances of the Polish National Theatre, directed by its creator Wojciech Bogusławski, on the Gdańsk stage were cultural events worthy of notice.

The fact that Napoleon lost the war with Russia resulted in the siege of Gdańsk in 1813. After a defence that lasted ten months, the Franco-Polish garrison capitulated. The city suffered serious damage: the suburbs were demolished again, many buildings in the western part of the city were demolished or burnt (among them the Dominican monastery) and 173 granaries and warehouses were burnt down, that is, approximately half the entire number within the old port on the Motława. This

The disastrous fire on Granary Island during the siege of the city in 1813, consumed 173 granaries

This lithograph by Helmsauer, made after a drawing by G. G. Ludvig, represents the mouth of the Vistula about 1825. In the foreground and on the right — the Wisłoujście Fortress (with the Baroque spire, from the first half of the 18th century). In the background — the sea and the mouth of the Vistula. On the left — the buildings of Nowy Port and the Port Canal marked by the masts of ships

was the heaviest loss for the besieged people, for the granaries which lay mainly beyond the range of contemporary artillery contained food supplies as well as other goods and a large proportion of the possessions of the inhabitants.

Johanna Schopenhauer wrote in her diary that the Gdańsk granaries were destroyed with the help

The 19th century saw the appearance of industrial plants based on a new source of power — steam. Sugar refinery on Granary Island

of rockets! Although this is not confirmed in other sources, it is a fact that incendiary rockets, known for a long time in Asia and brought to Western Europe by a British colonel called Congreve, were used during the siege of Gdańsk by both sides. The French used them to cannonade the British warships attacking Wisłoujście and the English who, it is said, brought three and a half thousand rockets, launched them onto the city. Therefore, one might say that it was only thanks to a happy coincidence

The levelling of fortifications near the Upland Gate in 1895. In the background — Torture Chamber and Prison Tower with a Renaissance (non-existent) spire

On the site of the former bastions, pseudo-Renaissance buildings were erected. By their size, they overwhelmed the Upland Gate (in the middle)

that Gdańsk avoided the fate of Copenhagen which was burnt in 1807 after a rocket attack by the British fleet.

As a result of flight, deportation, war losses, famine and disease — the population diminished to about 16,000, that is, to the figure for the beginning of the 15th century.

After Napoleon's fall, in spite of diplomatic missions by the inhabitants of Gdańsk, the Congress of Vienna decided to include Gdańsk once more in Prussia. Prussian administrators, as well as a large army garrison, again entered the town. From 1815 to 1825, Gdańsk was the capital of West Prussia. This brought an influx of German officials and this, taken together with the fact that many of the former inhabitants left the city, resulted to a large extent in the Germanization of the city. Wrzeszcz (without Strzyża Górna, Młynisk and Studzienka) was included in the administrative area of the city, and so were Nowy Port and Westerplatte, Siedlce, Chełm, Stare Szkoty and Oruńskie Suburb. The return of the former and the influx of new inhabitants caused an increase of the population of the city, including the suburbs, to 49,000, by the year 1819.

However, Gdańsk trade was declining. The reason was the abolition of the province of West Prussia in 1825 and the transfer of the provincial capital to Królewiec, the city's isolation from its natural hinterland by state boundaries, the high duties and, finally, failure to regulate the Vistula. Unemployment and poverty resulted in demonstrations by port workers.

The building of a network of roads, which was begun in the 1820's, could not improve the economic situation of the city, but it was changed by the coming of the railways. The first line, from the direction of Bydgoszcz and ending at a central station in Toruńska Street, was finished in 1852. In the 1860's, a branch line was built along the moat which was partly filled with earth but with its towers preserved as they were. This led to Nowy Port and, in 1870, a new branch was opened to Ko-

The buildings of the Technical University were also erected in pseudo-Renaissance, purportedly in "Gdańsk" style

In the 19th century, the one-storey, partly rural architecture of the suburbs began to give to Viennese Secession houses. Łączyńskiego Street in Nowy Port (Neo-Classical wooden house from about 1800)

Endeavours for the greatest possible exploitation of the land resulted in excessively dense and extremely unsound construction. This is what was concealed the historical façades of houses in the Main Town

szalin, with a station at Oliwska Gate. The present Central Station was not built until the end of the 19th century, after the towers that divided the railway line from the city were demolished (formerly a halt was located here, accessible from the present Trzeciego Maja Street).

The railway was one of the factors that fostered the development of the port. Others include the reduction of duties and the new mouth of the Vistula that came into existence in 1840. Together with the building of the floodgate in Płonia, it secured the port against floods and obstruction. After the disappearance of the old mouth, the island of Westerplatte became a peninsula and, despite its name, was now located to the east of the port entrance. The unnecessary floodgate which separated the Port Canal from the Vistula was demolished and the canal was later widened.

In 1879, a dock was built between Nowy Port and

Brzeźno and, ten years later, the left bank of the Dead Vistula, later known as Vistula Port was also adapted for use. In the first years of the 20th century, the present Kashubian Canal was built.

In 1840, industry based on new sources of energy began to develop in Gdańsk and this caused the decline of the water-mills at the Strzyża and Oliwski Stream. The first factories were armament plants; later, engineering factories were built, as well as chemical, food and timber works and rolling-stock factory and repairshop. The shipbuilding industry, which had old traditions in Gdańsk, was further expanded; new technological advances were introduced and, to a great extent, was turned over to the construction of warships. Two railway branch lines which crossed the town were built in the Dolne Miasto (Lower Town) to serve the industrial plants. In 1905, a railway line was completed to the factories on Ostrów Island, with a drawbridge

Factories badly located among dwelling houses in the Lower Town. On the left are found the preserved Baroque bastions; in the background — the Stone Sluice (as it looked in the 1920's)

on the Dead Vistula and a railway ferry across the Kashubian Canal.

Gdańsk was considered a fortress. For the numerous garrisons stationed in it, seven great complexes of barracks were built in the second half of the 19th century, five of them in the central area. At the beginning of the 20th century, two more groups of barracks were set up. The fortifications were modernized and new forts, coastal gun-emplacements and new reinforcements were constructed.

The development of the port and industry, the military garrisons and the increase of administrative personnel (after the province of West Prussia was again established with its capital in Gdańsk) caused an increase in the population to 109,000 in 1880, and 175,000 in 1910. Despite the Germanization campaign conducted by the Prussian authorities, and contrary to the official statistics, the strength of the Polish element began to increase. This was connected with the migration of the Kashubian population from the neighbouring areas to seek work in the factories and the awakening of their national consciousness. The existence of various Polish organizations and associations, and the publication, from 1891, of the *Gazeta Gdańska* (Gdańsk Newspaper) and many Polish books, confirm this fact.

At this time the suburbs expanded rapidly, especially Wrzeszcz which, in 1910, passed the 30,000 mark. Orunia, Siedlce and Nowy Port had approximately 10,000 inhabitants each, Oliwa was somewhat smaller; Stogi and Letnica had 3,100 inhabitants, and Brzeźno approximately 2,500.

The development of the suburbs could not have occurred without satisfactory transport facilities. In 1864, an omnibus from Gdańsk to Sopot was put into service and, eight years later, the first horse-drawn trams appeared. When, in the years 1895—1896, the trams were electrified, there were already lines to Wrzeszcz, Orunia and Siedlce, and two in the town-centre. In the last years of the 19th century, routes were opened to Nowy Port (along Wiślna Street), and, further on, through Brzeźno to

Wrzeszcz and, in 1901, to Wrzeszcz-Oliwa. In 1912, the road-bridge across the Dead Vistula was put into service, making Stogi and the whole of Zawiśle easily accessible.

In the 1860's work was begun on new water-mains and sewers. These were later rebuilt and modernized many times and formed a complicated network, with many junctures and pumping stations. In 1853, the first gas-works was built near the Stone Sluice and, 50 years later, when its output capacity was not sufficient, a much larger one was put up at Wałowa Street, and the old one demolished. In the last years of the 19th century, a power-station was built in Ołowianka.

The growing city was suffocating in its ring of fortifications which had lost their military significance. To facilitate transport, the gates were widened or demolished around 1870; later, parts of the ramparts were also pulled down. Complete demolition of the ramparts and towers was begun during the 1890's, mainly to gain new building-plots. Out of the twenty towers built in the 16th and 17th centuries, nine were demolished, including all on the western and northern sides of the city. The fortifications of Grodzisko and Biskupia Górka were preserved but sections, in the region of Oliwska, Siedlecka and Oruńska gates were demolished.

Building in the first half of the 19th century was restricted mainly to the reconstruction of houses that had been destroyed during the Napoleonic wars, which were often given a Neo-Classical appearance. Later, work was begun on new residential and public buildings. It is worth mentioning the buildings along the Jegiellonian Ramparts and Podwale Grodzkie Street, the whole complex at New Gardens, the present Świerczewskiego Street, the rebuilt Coal and Timber Markets, and a considerable part of Dolne Miasto, the Railway Company's Headquarters, the City Library, the National Archives, several school buildings, the Technical University and two hospital complexes in Wrzeszcz, buildings in Nowy Port, and the central parts of

In the absence of regulations on the protection of historical monuments, the owner's profit was the motive for the reconstruction and deformation of period houses. A part of the Long Shore

Wrzeszcz, Siedlce and Orunia. The buildings were in a variety of period styles — Neo-Gothic, Neo-Renaissance or Neo-Baroque — or even in no recognizable style at all.

The tendency to utilize space to the maximum, and the desire to make the greatest profit, led to extremely crowded and defective buildings and a mixture of residential buildings with factories and storehouses. In erecting new buildings, no consideration was given to their scale and their relation to the surroundings, so that in the historical sections, many valuable monuments were overshadowed or even concealed. Many old buildings were altered and some were demolished; buildings usually without any value from the architectural point of view were erected in their place (the market hall and the post office building on Długa Street). The terraces, so characteristic of Gdańsk, were demolished on almost all the streets, to facili-

The elimination of terraces characteristic of Gdańsk, changed the appearance of the streets. This is what Długa Street formerly looked like

Typical appearance of a street in the centre of Gdańsk at the beginning of the 20th century: Podwale Grodzkie — the section in front of the Main Station

tate traffic, though often when it was not really necessary.

When summing up this period in the history of Gdańsk, one must start from the fact that these were times of great change. The population increased rapidly, the suburbs developed, the port and industry expanded, city transport and municipal services were set up. However, when we take into account the fact that this took place during the period of industrial revolution and urban expansion, it is clear that, in comparison with other cities, Gdańsk did not expand very rapidly. In terms of population it fell to twentieth place among Prussian cities at the end of the 19th century compared with fourth place at the beginning of the 19th. It also declined from a leading port to an unimportant transloading centre. The fact that the city was cut off from its natural hinterland, its inconvenient geographical position in relation to the Prussian state, the widespread destruction during the Napoleonic wars, the military functions assigned to it, the changing decisions regarding its administration, and, at least during the first stage, the hostility of the Prussian authorities towards a city which had tried by all means to avoid Prussian rule — all this restricted the city's development in the 19th century.

Like so many other cities in the 19th century, a period of general decline in architecture and town planning, and of economic leissez-faire, Gdańsk underwent considerable economic development, while losing much of its architectural interest and cohesion.

FREE CITY

The Polish nation could not become reconciled to the partitions and the loss of independence, but force and the united action of the partitioning powers thwarted all attempts at regaining the latter. Not until the First World War, the quarrels of the partitioning powers and, later, the fall of the tsarist regime, was there a real opportunity to revive the Polish State.

The Polish question became a problem of international interest. One of the provisions which President Woodrow Wilson of the United States included in his fourteen-point declaration on the aims of the war was the creation of an independent Polish State with free access to the sea. This condition could be fulfilled only by including the mouth of the Vistula and Gdańsk within the Polish boundaries. And that is what the preparatory proposals at the peace conference in Paris stated. As a result of political speculations, however, the Treaty of Versailles only granted Poland a piece of barren seashore.

The same treaty established the "Free City of Gdańsk" at the mouth of the Vistula — an artificial political creation which was consigned to the care of the League of Nations. The Treaty of Versailles and the Paris Convention of November 9th, 1920, which resulted from it, guaranteed Poland many special rights and exceptional powers in the political and economic spheres. The Free City was included in the Polish customs area and Poland was to represent it in international relations and defend it against any possible aggression. Her exclusive rights to the Gdańsk port, also granted in the Versailles Treaty, were however limited in 1920. Under the Paris Convention, a Port and Water Routes Council was set up in which Poland only had a 50 per cent share. The representatives of the Free City of Gdańsk held the other half. Poland also received special rights as regards the railways, post office and telecommunication. The right to possess a separate area for transloading arms and munitions in Gdańsk port was important from the military point of view and the area set apart for this was Westerplatte. The Polish inhabitants of the Free City were guaranteed equal rights, including the right to have Polish schools and freedom of activity for Polish organizations.

The creation of the Free City was only a partial

The building which housed the Polish Railway Office and several Polish associations in the Free City of Gdańsk

A parade of Polish pathfinders from the Gdańsk Troop in the stadium of Wrzeszcz

solution. Despite the rights granted, it did not guarantee Poland fully free access to the sea and did not meet all her needs. As a result of this, the decision was taken to build a new port which would lie on Polish territory. Gdynia was one of the places considered suitable for this purpose. It was a fishing village which lay approximately 20 kilometres north of Gdańsk. The port built there was one of the most modern ones on the Baltic and in the world; as early as 1933 it handled more cargo than the port of Gdańsk and held first place among all the ports on the Baltic Sea. By 1939 the town built next to the port had a population of 120,000.

Even though the rival city of Gdynia had been built and despite later economic difficulties (the world crisis), the fact that Gdańsk was within the Polish economic sphere and connected with her vast hinterland created favourable conditions for her future growth. The port of Gdańsk was modernized and developed, with Poland covering more than half of the costs. Canals and docks, formerly never deeper than 7.5 metres, were deepened. Two new docks were built (at Westerplatte and a coal dock) and so were two transloading quays, so that the total length of quays increased to 31 kilometres compared with 21 kilometres previously. New warehouses, grain silos and tanks were built and the cargo-handling equipment increased from 26 to 98 items. The network of railways within the port was developed, to meet growing requirements. These investments made it possible to handle four times as much cargo and, thanks to this, in the years 1926—1932, Gdańsk was one of the main ports on the Baltic Coast. (It only later was outdistanced by Gdynia.)

Gdańsk industry also revived although to a lesser degree than the port. New factories set up included chemical, timber and office equipment plants. Some new factories made use of old army buildings left vacant as a result of the demilitarization of the Free City.

The development of the port and industry resulted in the foundation of many commercial, brokerage, transport, banking and other firms. There were over 40 Polish firms among them which played an important role in the economic life of Gdańsk (for example, in 1937 over 40 per cent of the cargo which passed through the port of Gdańsk was shipped by Polish firms). The revival of the economy caused the number of inhabitants to rise from 195,000 in 1921 to approximately 259,000 in 1936. However, this increase was only partly due to the general development because about 30,000 of the suburban population were included in the overall number of inhabitants after Oliwa (in 1926), Orunia, Olszynka, Brętowo and a few smaller settlements (in 1933) were included in the administrative boundaries of the city.

Many of the city's inhabitants were re-Polonized in the new political and economic situation. As a number of Germans also left the city and there was an influx of Poles, this brought the number of Polish inhabitants to approximately 50,000. The Polish Community Association of Poles was the largest Polish organization and numbered almost 40,000 members. The Association of Polish Scouts was particularly active, as were various glee and sports clubs. There were Polish newspapers and, in the scientific field, the Society of Friends of Science and Art active in Gdańsk published a *Gdańsk Yearbook*. Since the number and standard of the Polish schools maintained by the senate of the Free City was unsatisfactory, the Polish Mother School Organization organized private schools. Thanks to its activity, 20 nursery schools and 13 other schools were opened in the Free City, including seven primary, one secondary, two vocational and a music school.

The rights guaranteed Poland and the Polish inhabitants were not, however, fully respected and were even systematically restricted. Despite the city's interests and those of both its Polish and German inhabitants, chauvinistic elements provoked incidents. Excesses were repeatedly committed. Polish mail boxes were destroyed; Polish mailmen and customs inspectors were attacked; historical Polish

The building, pupils and teachers of the Polish Secondary School in Gdańsk

The houses in Marx Street in Wrzeszcz, one of the housing projects of the Free City period (photo from 1966, after reconstruction)

The housing of that period consisted for the most part of one-family houses, often situated on grounds without a sewage system. The Suchanin housing development; in the background — the school built after the war

eagles were broken off the Neptune Fountain; Polish students were expelled from the Technical University. After the government of the Free City was taken over by Hitler's followers, the National Socialists, the situation in Gdańsk began to become more and more strained, despite the officially correct relations between Poland and the Third Reich.

From the town-planning and architectural standpoints, no basic changes took place at that time in Gdańsk or, to be more exact, changes occurred within the area of the developing suburbs, and only to a small degree concerned the central part of the town. As a result of the demilitarization, army buildings and equipment were divided between Poland the municipal authorities. Even before the Free City was established in 1919 five outlying towers were demolished and so were the Oliwska and Siedlecka gates, together with the nearby rampart sections,

and, later, the ramparts at the former Oruńska Gate and the fort in Brzeźno. Part of the fortifications were adapted to recreational use. The army buildings later housed a variety of institutions, including the Polish post office, a Polish students' hostel and a Polish secondary school which was later rebuilt and extended.

Residential building was concentrated mainly in the area of northern Wrzeszcz and, to a somewhat lesser degree, in Siedlce, Suchanin and eastern Oliwa. Smaller settlements were set up on the eastern edge of the town centre, in Olszynka and Błonie, on the southern and western outskirts of Wrzeszcz, in Stogi and in a few other parts. The volume of building was not imposing. At the beginning, approximately 1,200 rooms were built per year, then this number diminished to about 800, so that in the years 1934—1939, altogether approximately 4,000 rooms were built. Small houses for one (71 per cent) or two families (approximately 23 per cent) predominated, many of them built of wood. The houses were built on large plots, included in areas that did not always have piped water or sewers and were sometimes even completely deprived of municipal services. Moreover, some of these settlements were built in unhealthly, damp districts, some of which even lay below sea level.

Progress in public building was very modest — during the years 1934—1939; that is, in the course of six years, altogether 17 buildings were erected. The more important of them include the extension of the Technical University and students' hostel in Siedlecka Street, two large schools in northern Wrzeszcz, a new tram-depot, the Social Insurance building in Wałowa Street and two cinemas in Elżbietańska Street. The cinemas were an example of the modernistic architecture which, during the 1920's, threatened to inundate the centre of town, even its most historic parts. Luckily, however, Gdańsk managed to defend itself against this threat and some conservation and cleaning works were undertaken. A few small churches were also built, mainly in the suburbs; among them was a Polish church erected in Pohulanka Street, on the boundary between the town centre and Siedlce. The second Polish church, St Stanislas, was housed in the former riding school of the barracks in Wrzeszcz.

A tram-line and a road along it, leading to the beach in Stogi, were built in 1927. Two years later, a tram-line to Nowy Port and a new street — today's Marynarki Polskiej Street — were completed (the former road to Nowy Port led along Wiślna Street and ran into the port functions). A few new tram-lines and roads were built and a small airport constructed between Wrzeszcz and Oliwa. A modern, sewage-farm, was opened in 1930 at Zaspa, which purified sewage from the north-western districts of Gdańsk and even from Sopot.

The city benefited from the construction of a number of sports centres, being in Wrzeszcz, on Smoluchowskiego Street.

THE CONFLAGRATION

The first shots or, at any rate, one of the earliest shots of the Second World War, were fired in Gdańsk. In view of this, the last war has sometimes been presented as a "war over Gdańsk" — but, is this true?

After the First World War, Germany was forced to return some of the territories that it had seized from its neighbours. The German nationalists and militarists were not resigned to this act of historical justice. Revanchist tendencies increased when Hitler, whose aim was German hegemony in Europe, came to power. Violating international treaties, as well as his own promises, Hitler's Third Reich created a powerful army, carried through the remilitarization of the Rhineland (1936), annexed Austria (spring, 1938), the Czech Sudeten region (autumn, 1938), the rest of Czechoslovakia (March 13th, 1939) and finally the Klaipéda district of Lithuania (March 23rd, 1939). The policy of appeasement that was supposed to save peace led Europe to the edge of a precipice. However, this was realized too late.

On April 28th, 1939, Hitler presented Poland with an ultimatum that infringed upon her sovereignty. Its terms included the annexation of Gdańsk. This ultimatum was rejected.

The autorities of the Free City, who were mainly Nazis, began to form SS divisions, which was contrary to the provisions of the Versailles Treaty on demilitarization. In face of the danger of a *putsch*, Poland strengthened the sentry division and armed the several dozen members of the staff at the post office. On August 25th, the old but modernized battleship *Schleswig-Holstein,* ostensibly a training ship, came to Gdańsk port to pay a "courtesy visit."

On September 1st the *Schleswig-Holstein* opened fire at dawn and at the same time the German army crossed the Polish border. This was not a local *putsch*, this was war! The German invasion of Poland brought England and France into the war, although at the beginning this was only a political gesture without any military consequences.

Two Polish outposts defended themselves in Gdańsk to their utmost ability: the Army Depot on Westerplatte and the Polish Post Office. The heroic post office personnel fought for more than ten hours,

At 4:45 a.m. on September 1 st, 1939, the German battleship *Schleswig-Holstein* paying a "courtesy visit" in Gdańsk, opened fire on Westerplatte

The garrison of the Polish Army Depot in Westerplatte, bombed from the land, sea and air and attacked by superior forces, defended themselves for seven days

although they were attacked by artillery and armoured cars. They surrendered only after the death of their commanding officer and after their building was set on fire by the Germans. They were not even granted a soldier's rights though they had defended a building that belonged to the Polish State, under the terms of international treaties. Of the entire staff of the Polish Post Office, only four men were able to save themselves by escaping at the moment the building surrendered. The rest were shot.

The unit of two hundred men at Westerplatte was attacked from land, sea and air. They were armed with three small calibre guns, four mortars, machine-guns and rifles. The reinforced guard-posts and barracks cellars only provided protection against shrapnel and small arms fire. But in face of the battleship *Schleswig-Holstein,* which was shelling them from a distance of a few hundred metres and which was armed with four 280 mm. and ten 150 mm. guns, as well as machine-guns, the defenders of Westerplatte were helpless. They were equally helpless in face of the artillery bombardment from Brzeźno and Wisłoujście, the heavy bombing attacks from the air, and the destroyers shelling them from off-shore. But even so, all the German attacks were repelled and Westerplatte did not capitulate until the seventh day, after most of the points of resistance had been destroyed and the unit that had been fighting without a break was utterly exhausted. At that time the German armoured divisions were already approaching Warsaw.

Then came the years of Nazi occupation. Only people who have lived through this nightmare know what it meant. The Gdańsk Poles learnt about it during the first hours of the war when all the leaders of the Polish community were arrested and imprisoned. Some of them were later murdered and the rest were sent to concentration camps. One of these camps was located in nearby Stutthof. It was set up on September 2nd and was at first intended mainly for Poles from the area of the Free City. In the years 1939—1945, approximateley 80,000 prisoners lost their lives there. Polish railwaymen,

At the same time, SS troops formed in the "demilitarized" Free City launched an attack on the Polish Post Office

customs officers, postmen, teachers, priests and members of Polish societies, and even young scouts, were persecuted and many of them died only because they had the courage to assert their Polish nationality in the "Free City" and to make use of the rights they were guaranteed by law.

During the first period of military successes, German town-planners worked out an ambitious plan for the development and rebuilding of Gdańsk. But

Chapel in St Mary's Church, dedicated to the memory of 2,214 Polish priests murdered or tortured to death in the years of Nazi occupation

The fortunes of war began to veer more and more. Even the German naval base, which had been transferred to Gdynia, far behind the lines and seemingly safe, became a target of Allied air raids. The raids caused widespread damage mainly within the port, and also sank several ships. The *Schleswig-Holstein* which had opened the Second World War by its shelling of Westerplatte was sunk in December, 1944. Although industrial plants in Gdańsk were for war production, including the building of

The Nazis rulers of Gdańsk were planning the construction of a huge complex of buildings for the gauleiter's seat and office on the hills near Oliwska Gate

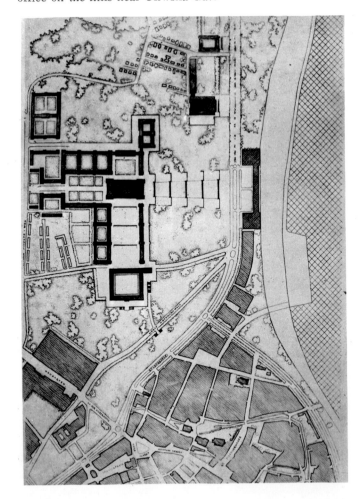

its implementation was limited to a small area of one of the planned districts (the settlement in Chełm), a few administrative buildings, a youth hostel on Biskupia Górka, and three small settlements in Siennicka Street in the town centre, in the present Wojska Polskiego Avenue in Wrzeszcz, and at the northern end of Grottgera Street in Oliwa. Apart from this, more than a dozen large reinforced concrete air raid shelters were put up. The temporary barracks set up for prisoners of war and foreign workers employed as slave labour were the very reverse of these shelters. Later, when retaliatory Allied air raids reached the German cities, barracks were also erected for the evacuated inhabitants from bombed territories. The great complexes of barracks, which were built even on the city lawns, became the dominating type of building in Gdańsk when it was annexed by the Reich. History made short shrift of the Nazis' plan.

In March 1945, German troops retreating from Gdynia blew up the quays and breakwaters of the port and, to block the port, sank in its entrance the damaged ship of the line *Gneisenau* (in the background)

submarines, it escaped large-scale destruction at that time.

In January, 1945, the great Soviet offensive across the Vistula got under way. The German inhabitants of Gdańsk began to escape in panic. A deep wedge, that reached the sea near Kołobrzeg, cut off the German armies in East Prussia and in Gdańsk Pomerania. The divisions that were pushed towards the sea gathered in the region of Gdańsk and Gdynia. The desperate rear-guard action was fought to enable the largest possible number of troops and inhabitants to be evacuated by sea. On March 23rd, Sopot was taken by the Soviet and Polish divisions, fighting together. They then launched an attack on the cities of Gdańsk and Gdynia.

The fall of Gdynia was hastened by the work of the Gdynia scouts, who supplied the Soviet high command with data on the German fortifications. Thanks to this, the city escaped large-scale destruction. Unfortunately, this did not apply to the port where special German divisions blew up everything

Troops of the Polish 1st Army in Długa Street. Such was the condition of Gdańsk at the time of its return to Poland

that could be destroyed, right up to the last moment.

After heavy fighting Gdańsk was captured on March 30th, 1945. After 126 years of German rule, interspersed by two episodes — Napoleon's Free City and the Free City of the League of Nations — the city, or to be more exact what remained of the city, returned to Poland.

RUINS AND RUBBLE

Bomb-blasted and shelled houses, stumps of wall silhouetted grotesquely against the sky, twisted girders, wrecked bridges, streets choked with rubble, trenches and barricades, the abandoned wrecks of tanks and cars and piles of military equipment — this is the picture of Gdańsk that those who saw it in 1945 will never forget. The scene was all the more desolate because certain parts of the town were completely deserted. For the careless passerby death lay in wait, in mines and live shells and hovered overhead, in walls that threatened to collapse at any moment.

Many weeks later the smell of burning and tendrils of smoke curling out of the ruins showed that fires were still smouldering under heaps of rubble or in buried cellars. Although the dead were collected and buried, in many places the smell of decomposing bodies showed that, under the rubble, there were still to be found the corpses of animals or human beings.

Sixty per cent of the city was destroyed. This included approximately 6,000 buildings, plus about 1,300 which were damaged. Many public buildings, including 33 schools, were demolished, burnt or seriously damaged. The city was covered with some three million cubic metres of rubble.

Transport was paralysed. Out of 36 of the larger bridges and viaducts, 20 had been blown up; included in this number were all the bridges on the Dead Vistula and the Motława and most of the railway viaducts. The railway lines were blocked by rubble. In many places the tracks had been torn up, the equipment devastated, installations destroyed and the buildings burnt (including the Central Station, the station in Wrzeszcz and the old station on Toruńska Street). The destruction of the street and tram network also was very serious. Of about 80 kilometres of tram tracks, approximately 15 per cent was destroyed, the traction grid literally had ceased to exist; half of the rolling-stock could not be even repaired and the rest had been destroyed in varying degrees.

Nearly two-thirds of the network of pipelines which had been about 320 kilometres long was also destroyed. Damage to the drainage system was less — about 15 per cent but of nine pumping stations only one was working, and the sewage-purification plant was devastated. Part of the installations of the gas works were destroyed and so were the gas mains in many places. The city was deprived of electricity as a result of the damage to the electric power station and power lines.

The destruction in the city was a result both of direct military action and of fires raging afterwards. Moreover, the German divisions tried to hold up the other side by blowing up important buildings before they could be taken by the Soviet and Polish armies. The destruction was not uniform, as it depended on the site of the main battles and the layout of the area. Comparatively little damage was suffered by less densely built up peripheral areas such as the south-western outskirts of Wrzeszcz, Suchanin, the outskirts of Orunia and Brzeźno, almost the whole of Oliwa, the central and northern parts of Wrzeszcz, especially in the neighbourhood of Grunwaldzka Street and Siedlce. The central and northern parts of Orunia, Stogi and Nowy Port were destroyed to a much greater degree. However, the worst devastation was concentrated in the town centre. This was due to its strategic siting, the density of building and the large amount of timber used in the construction of the historic old houses. The destruction in the central district reached 90 per cent and, in some parts of special distinction it was almost total.

The whole historic district and especially the Main Town, Old Town, Old Suburbs and Granary Island looked like a sea of ruins with more massive walls standing out, here and there, and an occasional building that had miraculously survived. But the picture was constantly changing: the greatest devastation was wrought by fire. Therefore, at first, most of the burnt-out shells of buildings remained standing, until they finally collapsed under the bufetting of strong winds and added to the rest of the rubble. The devastation wrought by war was continued by nature. It was impossible to prevent this during the first, most difficult period of total reconstruction after the war. To be more exact —

some preventive measures were taken but these were necessarily very limited at the beginning, so that only the most valuable buildings could be saved. On the other hand, some of the walls that threatened to collapse had to be demolished for reasons of safety.

Within the centre of town, several hundred Gdańsk burghers' houses suffered destruction; many of them were of great architectural interest. These included such famous buildings as the Uphagen House, the Ferber House, the Lion's Castle at Długa Street, the Angel (or English) House at Chlebnicka Street and the Golden House at Długi Targ Street, of which only part of the front wall was saved. Of the whole Main Town only a complex of houses within the region of St John's Church and single burghers' houses at Szeroka and Ogarna Streets were preserved, although they too were damaged. Only one house remained in the Old Town — the Renaissance Mansion of the Pelplin Abbots, located on the Radunia Canal. A few of the more interesting houses remained among the 19th century buildings in the region of Osiek and Grodzka Streets in the Old Suburb near Wałowy Square and near the Holy Trinity Church. Larger groups without value from the architectural point of view survived in the Lower Town and at the foot of Biskupia Górka.

Of the old historic granaries, two — the "Wisłoujście" (53 Chmielna Street) and "Nowa Pakownia" on Szafarnia Street — were only slightly damaged. Of all the rest, only burnt-out walls and rubble remained.

The fortified buildings which had thicker walls and were more massive, and also some public buildings and churches, were preserved in a somewhat better state; however, here too destruction was great. All the Gothic gates and towers and also the Green and Golden gates were burnt and partially destroyed by gun-fire. The Lowland and Żuławska gates within the ring of the more modern fortifications suffered less damage.

Only the damaged external walls remained of the finest example of the Gdańsk Renaissance style —

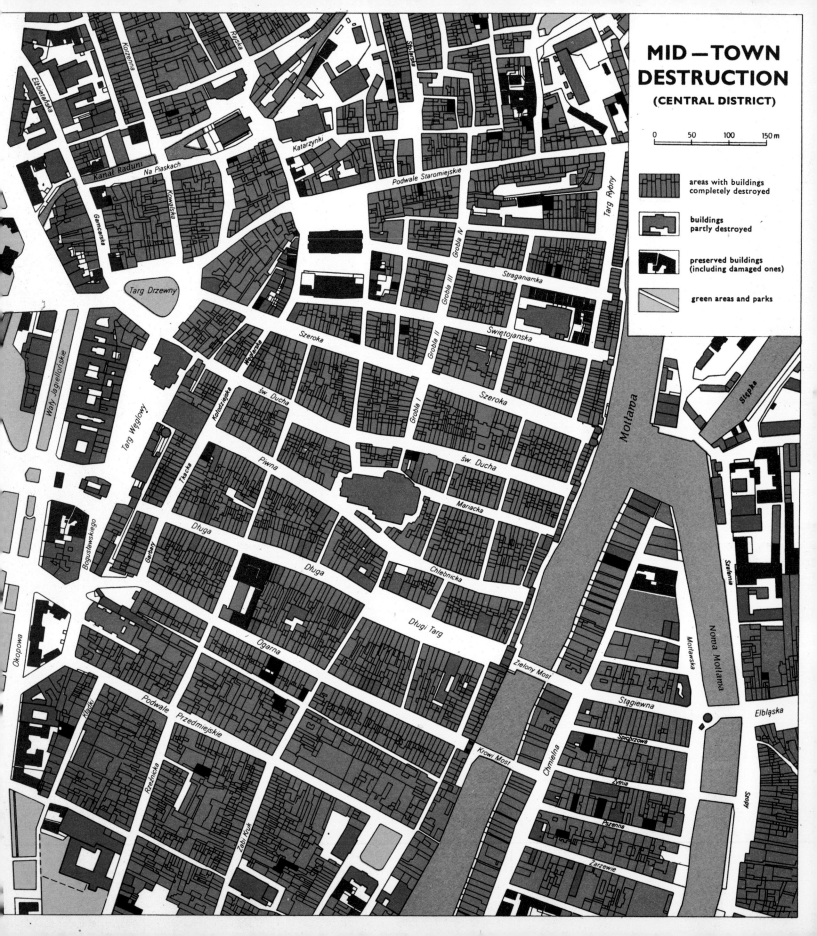

MID—TOWN DESTRUCTION
(CENTRAL DISTRICT)

0   50   100   150 m

areas with buildings completely destroyed

buildings partly destroyed

preserved buildings (including damaged ones)

green areas and parks

Elżbietańska
Kozienna
Rajska
Sukienna
Kanał Raduni
Na Piaskach
Katarzynki
Kowalska
Gancarska
Podwale Staromiejskie
Targ Rybny
Targ Drzewny
Grobla IV
Straganiarska
Grobla III
Grobla II
Szeroka
Świętojańska
Wały Jagiellońskie
Korzenna
św. Ducha
Grobla I
Szeroka
Targ Węglowy
Thcka
Piwna
św. Ducha
Motława
Stępka
Mariacka
Bogusławskiego
Długa
Gdańsk
Garbary
Długa
Chlebnicka
Szafarnia
Okopowa
Długi Targ
Nowa Motława
Ogarna
Motławska
Zielony Most
Stągiewna
Elbląska
Kletki
Podwale Przedmieskie
Chmielna
Spichrzowa
Rzeźnicka
Krowi Most
Żytnia
Szopy
Żabi Kruk
Pszenna
Zarzewie

Stumps of scorched walls projecting towards the sky...
This is what the Green Gate looked like in 1945

Streets covered by heaps of rubble, and walls that could collapse at any moment, made moving about the city difficult. The Słodowników Street area; in the background — the tower of the Main Town Hall

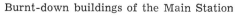

Burnt-down buildings of the Main Station

Railway communication was paralyzed. The destroyed engine-shed and engine-house

The centre of the city was destroyed by more than 90 per cent. Parts of houses in Kotwiczników Street

the Great Arsenal. The Big Mill and the Small Arsenal were in a similar plight. In the Artus Court not much remained beyond the walls and a piece of ceiling, supported by three columns damaged by fire. The Main Town Hall lost its roof, chiming and cupola; the interior was burnt out and the walls damaged by shells. The headquarters of the Natural Science Society at Długie Pobrzeże were seriously damaged. The thick walls of the Medieval Crane, the Żuraw, were damaged and its wooden works burnt. The House of the St George Fraternity and the pseudo-classic theatre building at the Coal Market went up in flames, and so did the Gothic rectory of St Mary's Church and, almost all the monastery buildings.

On the whole, the thick walls of the churches

The Main Town from the side of the Motława

Standing out here and there amidst the ruins were the walls of the more solid buildings or of those which luckily escaped destruction. St Mary's Church as seen through the ruins of Piwna Street

Although the walls of the church suffered only minor damage, it was badly destroyed all the same: the roofs were consumed by fire, half of the vaults collapsed and the others threatened to follow suit

proved most resistant to the destructive force of shells and flames, but almost all of them lost their roofs and vaults, either entirely or in part. Half the vaults in St Mary's collapsed, the rest were damaged. In the Church of SS. Peter and Paul a few pillars collapsed, as well as the ceilings. St Catherine's Church lost its ceilings, roofs, a beautiful Late Renaissance cupola and chimes that played a tune; the gables of the eastern wall collapsed later. Those completely burnt include the churches of St Barbara, St Bartholomew, the Holy Ghost and St Joseph, while St Elizabeth's was partly burnt. Only the tower remained of the Saviour's Church at Zaroślak and the Royal Chapel was badly damaged. Happily the

churches of St Nicholas, Corpus Christi, together with the former hospital building, St James' Church, rebuilt in the 19th century, and — of the secular buildings — the Old Town Hall escaped serious damage.

Historic buildings outside the central district also did not escape destruction. The former Abbots' Palace in Oliwa and part of the monastery buildings were burnt and the former Cistercian Church (now Cathedral) lost its tall spires. Manor houses at Zaspa and one in Polanki were also destroyed. The central and oldest part of the unique port fortress in Wisłoujście was seriously damaged.

Gdańsk industry suffered great losses. The build-

Industrial plants were destroyed or devastated. This is what the grounds of the Gdańsk Shipyard looked like at the time

ings suffered less damage on the whole than the machinery and plant. In the Gdańsk Shipyard, for instance, damage to buildings amounted to 30 per cent but to machinery 70 per cent.

Gdańsk port was inaccessible to shipping, although the quays were relatively little damaged (about 15 per cent). The entrance to the port was blocked by the ship *Africana* and the wrecks of 60 ships, cars, boats and equipment blocked the canals and dock basins. Mines presented a serious danger, as did sunken consignments of ammunition and explosives. Nearly half the cargo-handling machinery was completely destroyed and the rest was damaged. Warehouse losses were even greater, almost reaching 90 per cent.

Despite the scale of the destruction the port of Gdańsk was in a much better state than of Gdynia. The German army systematically blew up nearly all its breakwaters (90 per cent) and half its quays (6 kilometres); the rest were seriously damaged. Of the cargo-handling machinery only half was even worth repairing. Warehouses suffered comparatively less damage but, even here, a quarter were wiped out. The wrecks of dynamited cranes, ships, machinery, quantities of explosives, mines, etc., blocked the dock-basins. The entrance to the port was blocked by the *Gneisenau* (31,800 tons). In contrast to the port, the city of Gdynia escaped comparatively lightly. Destruction was estimated at approximately 17 per cent, but transport facilities were severely affected (viaducts were blown up).

The town to suffer least damage (10 per cent) was Sopot.

Damage to the dikes and the destruction of the pumping station in Żuławy meant that 72,000 hectares of land were flooded and tens of thousands more, including land to the east of Gdańsk, were turned into a swamp. This was another serious problem that had to be tackled in order to put the Gdańsk region back on its feet again.

PRESENT

LIFE RETURNS

Liberated Gdańsk was not only destroyed but, to a large degree, also deserted. On September 1st, 1939, it had a population of 247,000 and during the war years even more. As a result of the evacuation imposed by the German authorities, and partly due to the exodus of inhabitants and the war losses, this figure was greatly diminished. According to Kryński *, in April, 1945, there were approximately 139,000 inhabitants in Gdańsk but in comparison with other data, this figure seems too high. Perhaps it included not former inhabitants but also refugees from other than German areas, and even prisoners and workers of other nationalities that were used for forced labour. After liberation, these people began to leave the city and went to their homelands. This caused a further large decrease in the population. Also some inhabitants of German nationality decided to leave; among them women and old people were predominant. In the second half of 1945, after the Potsdam Conference, the deportation of the remaining Germans was carried out. But this did not cause a further decrease in the number of inhabitants because the diminution was counterbalanced by the influx of Poles.

Battles with German armies that were surrounded on Sobieszewska Island and on Hel Peninsula were still going on when the first operating groups of Polish reconstruction specialists arrived in Gdańsk. The smoke of fires that had not yet been put out was still rising to the sky. The specialists' task to organize the city administration, protect property, operate communication lines, ports and industry and, finally, rebuild the city, seemed beyond human ability. The conditions of work in the city were extremely difficult since it was without communication, water, gas and electricity. Literally everything was scarce or lacking: food and tools, means of transport and hands to work. People often worked alone or in small groups, undertaking tasks normally performed by a dozen men or sometimes by several dozen. This work was undertaken in a period of post-war confusion when the administration was just being organized and often could

---

* Henryk Edel Kryński, *Województwo Gdańskie. Studium Społeczno-gospodarcze* (Gdańsk Voivodship. A. Socio-economic Study), *Wydawnictwo Morskie,* Gdynia, 1961.

The first trains in the Main Station. On the left — ruins of houses in Podwale Grodzkie Street

Putting railways into service required the reconstruction, and in some cases the removal, of destroyed viaducts. This one blocked the Wojska Polskiego Street between Wrzeszcz and Oliwa

assure neither effective help nor necessary security. Despite this, the early difficulties were overcome with the help of the Soviet and Polish military authorities.

The number of inhabitants grew constantly. It is difficult to state at present how many Poles were in Gdańsk at the moment of liberation. During April, as Ziomek* has calculated, 3,200 people arrived in the city and later, from a few thousand to over ten thousand every month. Approximately 70,000 Poles had come to Gdańsk by the end of 1945. People from various parts of Poland were among

* Maksymilian Józef Ziomek, *Przemiany demograficzne w Polsce Ludowej na obszarze województwa gdańskiego* (Demographic Changes in People's Poland within Gdańsk Voivodship), *Gdańskie Towarzystwo Naukowe*, Gdańsk, 1965.

them. Often they had been deprived of their homes and places of work by the war and occupation. They were freed prisoners-of-war, prisoners from concentration camps, people repatriated from the USSR and other countries, and also inhabitants of the neighbouring Kashubian region.

The city returned to life and life even began to become normal, despite the great devastations and various difficulties that came from all sides. Two weeks after the city was taken, and while war activity was still taking place, on April 13th, 1945, school registration was announced. This is a specific demonstration which expresses the mood prevailing at the time. Twenty-one school buildings, the least

The city began to return to life but its completely ruined centre remained dead for a long time

destroyed, were prepared for use and, in May, 1945, 616 pupils began to study in them.

One of the most important tasks was to reactivate the lines of communication. On the evening of April 3rd, a train formed in Bydgoszcz, carrying a labour group of 180 railwaymen, reached Orunia. A week later, the first train passed through Gdańsk to Gdynia and in May passengers could travel to Wejherowo. The complete reactivating of the junction involved clearing the fallen viaducts off the tracks and rebuilding bridges and other constructions. One of the last sections, the line to Przeróbka, was reopened in August, 1945. The work on the steets and roads was begun by filling in craters, clearing away rubble, mines and barricades, provisional repairing of bridges or replacing them with ferries, repairing viaducts and organizing substitute detours.

The city, deprived of water, was threatened with an epidemic and this is why special efforts were undertaken to put the water conduits into opera-

Reconstruction began from the most precious historical monuments, such as St Mary's Church and the Main Town Hall. In 1949 their roofs were repaired and the reconstruction of the spice on the Town Hall tower was started

Reconstruction of the Renaissance House of the Natural Science Society (now the Archaeological Museum)

tion. On May 19th, water from the first pump reached some of the pipes. A month later, the electric power-station began working. In July, the first trams set out on their routes, at first on only one line (Oliwska Gate — Wrzeszcz), on a single track. The port of Gdańsk started operating in the same month — four cranes were set to work and on July 11th, the first post-war ship was serviced; it was the Finnish *Imo Ragnar*. At the same time, the Railway Stock Repairing Plant began operating.

Later, every month, even every week, brought new, happy events: production was begun in the Railway Stock Industrial Plant, further sections of the communication lines began operating, the public utility system and equipment were repaired, the buildings were redecorated. Although each of these events might seem like a trifle, especially from the perspective of years, their sum meant bringing Gdańsk back to life. At the beginning, it was exactly these, sometimes not very spectacular achievements, which created the basis for further successes.

The city was coming back to life, but the devastated centre of town was still lifeless. The following problem had to be considered: what should be done with the mid-town and other areas of total destruction? Both the extent of devastation, as well as the lack of belief that it would be possible to recapture what ages had created, caused voices to be raised demanding that the centre of town should not be rebuilt but should remain in ruins, testimony to the former splendour of Gdańsk and the barbarity of war.

A significant factor in these proposals was the awareness that the conditions that had shaped Gdańsk had changed and that these changes called for a different solution to certain problems. And, in reality, these changes were important, with regard to political relations as well as economic and social conditions. The Free City had ceased to exist, and Gdańsk had again become part of the Polish Republic and had thus regained its whole hinterland. However, at the same time, the building of the port and city of Gdynia between the world wars and

Nearly all the period houses of the Main Town had to be rebuilt from foundations like these houses in Długa Street. In the background — the Golden Gate and the Prison Tower

In that stage of reconstruction, the characteristic gables of the houses on Piwna Street already began to come into view

the fact that Poland had regained the lands on the Baltic Coast that once belonged to the Piast dynasty, deprived Gdańsk of her former monopolistic position in serving Polish ocean commerce. Nationalizing the economy and introducing planning on a large scale were further changes that occurred at that time.

Also the changes that concerned the municipality itself were important. For centuries, until the end of the 19th century, Gdańsk was the only city within this area and its development took place by the addition of new districts along a network of streets that emerged from the centre of town. Therefore, this was a concentric structure and the only deformations were caused by the irregularities of the ground. This basic shape was not changed in the 20th century by the fact that Sopot was transformed into a municipal centre nor even by the fact that a new large port and municipal centre — Gdynia, although cut off by the country's old frontier, was created.

Although the development of Gdynia took place under different conditions, it followed a similar course to that of Gdańsk. Suburbs, that crystallized the earliest, began to grow up around the centre.

Here also, as in Gdańsk, the transportation system had the form of rays emerging from the centre, deformed by natural conditions. An almost complete lack of circular connections and lines that would tie the suburbs to each other without running through the centre of town, was a characteristic feature of both these forms, which resulted only partly from the natural conditions and to a much larger extent from insufficient planning and investment. A two-track railway and a road with one line of traffic in each direction were the only connections between these two forms.

After the war, these two forms, which were established independently of each other, suddenly faced a situation in which they not only had to cooperate but in which one large spatial entity began to form. This was caused by the frontier having disappeared and that both of the cities, and their ports, were under common administration and planning, and also by the destructions of war. As a result, the voivodship authorities were first located in Sopot; Gdynia was the services and cultural centre, and Wrzeszcz, which was less destroyed and had more inhabitants, took on the role of a substitute centre for Gdańsk.

Thus, a completely new division of management and service centres, of places of work and residence was made. As a result, there were traffic routes and communication needs which were different from those formerly existing. And although it was known that some of these changes were of a transitional character, and that many anomalies would disappear together with rebuilding, it was also beyond doubt that the structure that would be formed would be a new organized area, completely different from what had previously existed here.

Therefore, rebuilding could not depend only on what had existed before. The spatial structure had not only to be rebuilt but also transformed so that it could be adapted to the needs of the new unit that was only being made. What would this unit be like?

REASON MUST PREVAIL

Cities — their network of streets, the underground pipelines and buildings — are all extermely durable elements that are difficult to transform. We can find evidence of this in the structure of streets of towns that are hundreds of years old, and have hardly changed at all during that time. Also, there are sometimes almost unsurmountable difficulties in rebuilding districts that have been badly planned and built. Therefore, when planning a city, not only the current needs should be considered, but the plans should reach into the future, at least 20 to 30 years.

In a country devastated by war and in its ruined cities which were busy solving current problems, sometimes with extreme difficulty, it was not easy to accept this principle. Therefore, such ideas were expressed as that the main centre of the whole complex should be maintained in Sopot and that the status quo that had come into being as a result of the war devastations should be accepted or that the centre of Wrzeszcz should be rebuilt as Gdańsk's mid-town. Some activists from Gdynia proposed that Gdańsk should not be rebuilt; they were interested only in developing a more modern Gdynia. This was caused not only by their feeling for their own city but also by their incomprehension of some of the more general problems.

The proper plans for spatial administration were worked out almost from the first days after liberation. This was possible due to the fact that the people who were entrusted with organizing the spatial planning centres came to Gdańsk with the first operational groups. The first town planning designs that were supposed to satisfy current needs, as for example widening Grunwaldzka Street, were made in the Planning Department of the Municipal Government under the direction of Professor Władysław Czerny. He also made the first plan for rebuilding the centre of Gdańsk. At the same time, a project for administering the region was worked out under the direction of Professor Stanisław Różański in the Regional Directorate of Spatial Planning. Within the Regional Directorate, the "Gd Plan Office" was set up, it was directed by the architect Kamil Lisowski and in the years 1946—1948 this office worked out a plan for administration of the port and municipal complex of Gdańsk-Gdynia.

The afore-mentioned plans determined the main

functions of the city. They finally fixed the location of the main centre of the complex in the middle of Gdańsk; they indicated the main directions of development of the ports, industry and residential districts and the principles of the communication structure. At the same time, the need was noted to build an electric railway on separate tracks to connect the cities belonging to the complex, and to build new roads, including an express highway along the complex.

The plan of the port and municipal complex of Gdańsk-Gdynia was worked out for the period up to 1975. The main points of the plan can be summarized in the following way: the complex contained Gdańsk and Gdynia, and Sopot which lies between them, also Pruszcz and Rumia situated on the edges of the complex. The further development of the complex should be linear due to the natural conditions. The complex should have two distribution and service centres — the main one in the mid-town of Gdańsk and a subsidiary one in Gdynia, giving the port of Gdańsk greater possibilities for development. The most advantageous population of the complex was figured to be between 650,000 and maximum of 800,000. Gdańsk itself was designed to house 300,000 inhabitants, of which 50,000 were to live in the centre of town, 70,000 in Wrzeszcz, 44,000 in Siedlce, 37,000 in Oliwa, 36,000 in Orunia and 20,000 in Stogi. The plan located the distribution and service centre in the northern part of the Gdańsk mid-town and proposed its further development (the port and municipal distribution centre) through the areas bordering on the two shipyards then existing, to the area of Ostrów Island that was then not fully made use of. This was an attempt to bring the centre of town closer to the port which had moved closer to the sea in the 19th and 20th centuries. But the next few years proved that this attempt was not realistic. The development of the shipbuilding industry made it impossible — development to an extent that no one then predicted.

At the same time that general plans were being worked out, particular plans for those parts of the city that were expected to be reconstructed rapidly were being realized. A section of the mid-town adjoining the Main Station and called "Gdańsk 1946—1947" was one of these districts. The architects Władysław Czerny, Witold Kuczewski and Wacław Tomaszewski were its designers. Three of the four buildings planned were erected, among them the present Monopol Hotel; the skyscraper that was to have been built north of the hotel was not erected. As a result of later changes in the plans, the architects decided not to build it, though in a rather odd way; it did enter into the history of post-war Gdańsk city planning. While the hotel was being built, one of the local journalists wrote that a skyscraper was going up. So, when four storeys of the building, 100 metres long, were completed, the misled inhabitants christened the hotel with the name of "horizontal skyscraper."

The reconstruction of Główne Miasto (Main Town) was especially carefully prepared. After introductory drawings were made by the architects Witold Doliński, Stanisław Bobiński and Władysław Czerny and plans by the general conservation expert, the Design and Research Office, directed by the architect Zbigniew Żuławski, took over further work.

The plans for the centre of town were worked over many times. For instance, two competitions were held, in 1950 and 1951. About 30 architects worked on the subject, not counting designers specializing in other fields. The best detailed plan for the whole mid-town was worked out in the years 1951—1952 by Leszek Dąbrowski, Adam Kühnel and Witold Rakowski. It was accepted, together with a new version of the general plan of the Gdańsk-Gdynia complex, by the Presidium of the Government in 1952. In this plan the development of the shipbuilding industry was finally taken into consid-

This view of the Main Town is a model, one of those which served to check the correctness of town-planning concepts

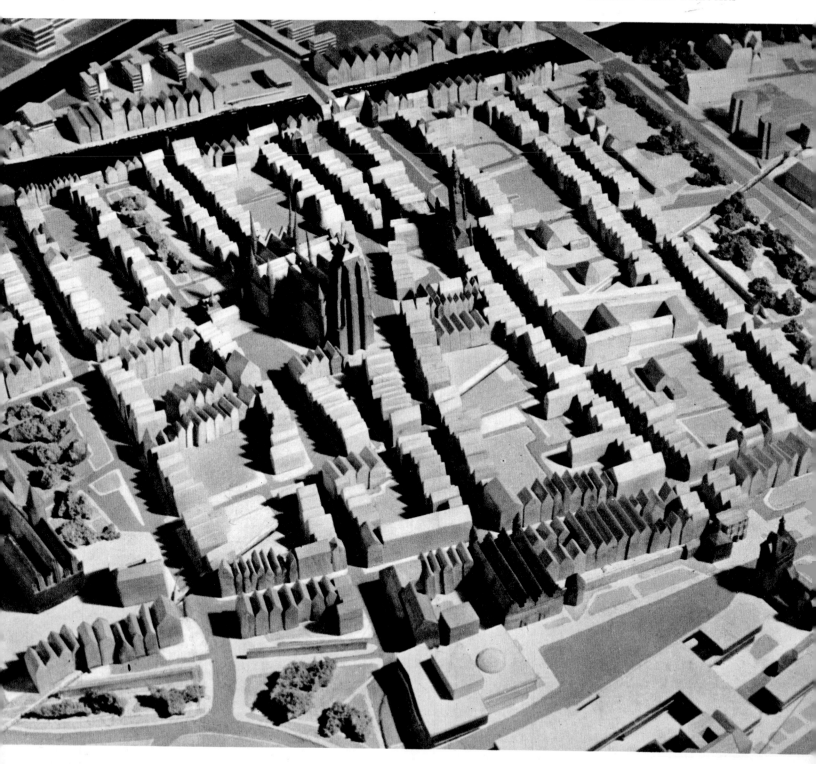

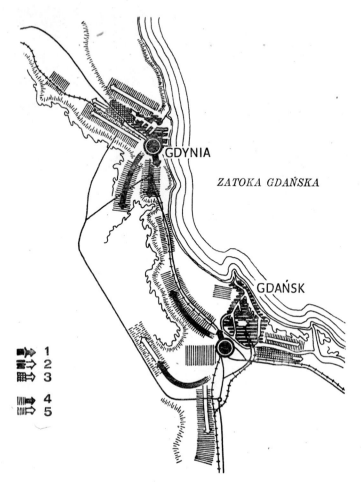

ZATOKA GDAŃSKA

GDYNIA

GDAŃSK

1
2
3
4
5

Reconstruction consisted not only of rebuilding what had been in existence before. Simultaneously, projects and studies for scores of years in the future were undertaken. This is how in 1947 in the "Gd Town Planning Office" the direction of the development of the Gdańsk-Gdynia urban complex was specified: 1. Municipal centres 2. Port areas 3. Industrial areas 4. Housing developments for workers employed in centres 5. Housing developments for workers employed in industry and ports

the fact that a new filling station was to be built beyond the city, a compositional axis was planned to run from the Main Station to Polski Hak. It was planned to intersect the industrial and port belt of many kilometres with recreational green areas and sport equipment, between Polski Hak and Siennicki Bridge.

The general plan mentioned above, which was designed by a group directed by the architect Stefan Lier, became the basis for the plans of a few districts: Orunia (architect Maria Klajbor), Siedlce and Oliwa (architect Wiesław Gruszkowski) and Wrzeszcz (architect Irena Heilman). The plan of reconstruction for the destroyed, central part of Wrzeszcz or, rather, the plan of building it anew, was worked out by a team of young Gdańsk architects: Roman Hordyński, Daniel Olędzki, Konrad Pławiński, Jerzy Poklewski and Romuald Szurowski. The plan for this part of the city, called the Grunwald Housing Development was almost completely realized, although with many later changes, the main point of which was the introduction of single buildings, 11 to 17 storeys high. In the mid-town, after another competition in 1953, detailed plans were made for the northern part including the former Old Town, and for the southern part — Stare Przedmieście (the Old Suburbs). The first was designed by the architects Danuta Weirowska and Witold Rakowski, with the cooperation of Leszek Dąbrowski, and the second by the architects Roman Hordyński, Tadeusz Lepczak, Daniel Olędzki, Danuta Weirowska and the engineer Włodzimierz Zamorski.

Economic changes required a revision of the city plans. In this connection, the preparation of a new version of the general plan of the Gdańsk-Gdynia complex became one of the main tasks of the Voivodship City Planning Office that was set up in 1955. This plan was worked out in 1957—1960, with the cooperation of numerous specialists. The team of designers consisted of the architect Bohdan Szermer, Adam Sokół, the engineer Jan Siczek, Józef Nieroda, the architects Zbigniew Czernichowski, Ro-

eration and its designers gave up the idea of crowding part of the mid-town district into the shipyard area. On the other hand, an administrational-cultural centre was designed in the western part of the mid-town, at Podgórze. In connection with

The authors of the project and conception works made various propositions with regard to the localization and layout of the new centre.

Here are some examples: A — architect S. Rychłowski, 1950; B — architects: L. Dąbrowski and S. Różański, 1950; C — architects: W. Lew, S. Koziczuk and J. Chmiel, 1950; D — architects: K. Lisowski and W. Spisacki, 1951; E — architect: W. Minkiewicz, 1952; F — architects: L. Dąbrowski, A. Kühnel and W. Rakowski, 1952.

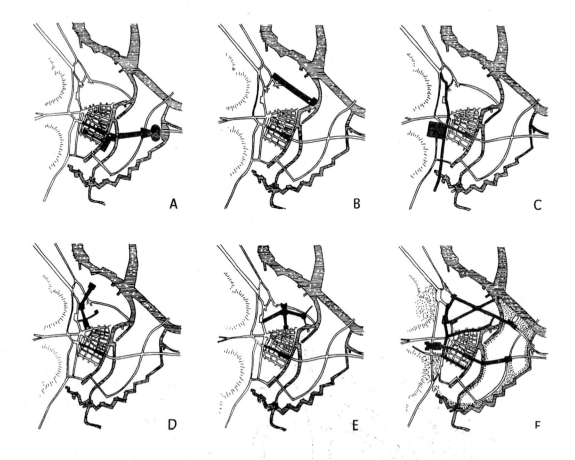

muald Szurowski, Stanisław Tomaszek, Wiesław Gruszkowski and the engineer Jan Bogusławski. The proposals for the plan were accepted by the Council of Ministers and the plan itself was approved by the county authorities in 1962. According to this plan, the number of inhabitants of the whole municipal complex was to be 800,000 in 1980 and of Gdańsk 390,000, or over 90,000 more than in the "Gd Plan" of 1948. There were characteristic changes in the numbers of inhabitants planned for the following districts: for the mid-town a reduction of 15,000 and for Oliwa an increase of almost 30,000. The first resulted from the necessary increase in the programme of services and of communication areas in the mid-town, the second was connected with finding the areas of Przymorze that were convenient to build upon. There were proposals to locate the rest of the new inhabitants in two new districts in higher land: Piecki and Ujeścisko-Łostowice.

But the most important decisions contained in the plan were: preserve large development reserves for the ports, priority for the shipbuilding industry and the sea economy closely connected with it, a certain necessary spreading out of other fields of that industry, recognizing tourism as one of the elements that build the city complex, and accepting the principle of increasing employment in the services (laundry, repairs, etc.) until it would equal employment in industry. These principles were later

Models constructed for the various parts of the Main Town already gave an idea of the architectural character of the buildings planned

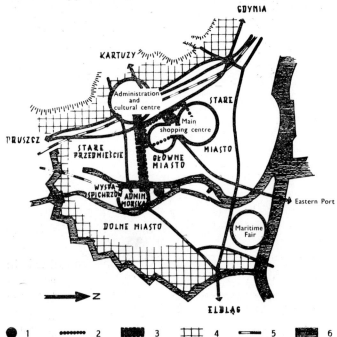

Functional scheme and model of the mid-town, according to the plan from 1963:
1. Travel Offices; 2. Street shopping line; 3. Main compositional axis of administrative and cultural functions 4. Municipal green areas; 5. Railway line; 6. Water System

affirmed in the plan for development of the port, and the policy of spreading industry was accepted by the administrative authorities.

The principle of a semi-belt form was maintained in the spatial structure, and the number of inhabitants planned for the Pruszcz-Rumia belt increased from the 620,000 anticipated for 1948 to 730,000. However, it was stated that later this structure should begin to take on a constellational form. In this connection, two exterior districts, not quite aptly called satellite towns, were planned on the higher land beyond the forest belt. The necessity to further decentralize the centres was acknowledged. Thus, besides the main management and service centre in the Gdańsk mid-town and a subsidiary one for the northern part of the complex in Gdynia, a main centre of the tourist movement in Sopot and a centre for serving agriculture in Pruszcz were planned. Also the necessity of building a new airport was anticipated on an area formerly planned as residential and a large complex of service centres, including a large shopping centre, were foreseen.

The problems of communication and municipal

Model for the detailed plan of the centre of Gdańsk. In the foreground — the Lower Town; in the background — the Chełm and Grodzisko hills

engineering were very carefully analyzed since, in the complicated conditions of the Gdańsk-Gdynia complex, these might be most important in deciding the direction of development or even in limiting it. Further expansion of the local network of electric railways was planned and decisions taken regarding the size of the districts that would fit the communication service and water supply. The locations of green areas in the previous plans were maintained, that is, to keep the park and forest areas on the upland and join them to the green at the seashore by diagonal belts. But these belts were

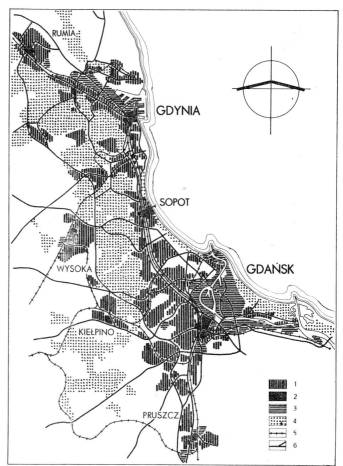

Sketch of the plan of the general Gdańsk-Gdynia complex, worked out in 1957—1960 for the year 1980.
1. Areas for housing construction; 2. Main service centres 3. Port and industrial areas 4. Forests 5. Railway lines 6. Main streets and roads

limited and their form precisely given and, as far as possible, they were located on areas that were not convenient for building. To tie the city with the sea in composition, several proposals were made, mainly for the area between Wrzeszcz and the attractive and picturesque region around the entrance to the port. Also exhibition and fair areas were proposed that could become a functional and compositional link between the middle of town and the port (sea fairs).

The plan was the basis for working out the details for more than ten districts, among which one should first mention that for the centre of Gdańsk, worked out in the Municipal City Planning Workshop by a team consisting of the architects Irena Balcerkiewicz and Stanisław Michel and the engineer Tadeusz Woronowicz.

Both the changes and a more precise description of the economic tasks, adding details to the analysis and studies and also changes in the obligatory rules and norms, required constant work on the plans, as well as bringing them up to date from time to time. To make sure that the concepts for the future were correct, in 1962 directional studies in their most general outline, reached approximately to the year 2000. Three variants of this study were worked out by the architects Wiesław Gruszkowski, Stanisław Tomaszek and Bohdan Szermer. Also, the analysis of the natural conditions and technical studies was deepened and now, once again, the team's plan will be brought up to date. The plans must guarantee conditions for broad development; the possibility of meeting both present and future needs. Reason must prevail and lead to the future!

RESTORED BEAUTY

During the history of Gdańsk, which existed for ages, and mainly in the period of its greatest splendour, hundreds of beautiful buildings were erected: they formed a harmonious complex of unusual quality. Many buildings were demolished in the 18th and 19th centuries and some parts were defaced by improper alterations. Also some parts of the historical complex were deformed when new, styleless or even just plain ugly buildings hid or overshadowed the historical buildings. But, despite this fact, Gdańsk still had the reputation of a beautiful city. Because, in reality, despite neglect and deformation, it was beautiful, though with the sad beauty that remains from former splendour.

However, the year 1945 finally came, the last year of the most cruel war in history. Part of the price that Gdańsk paid was that its monuments were reduced to ashes. Let us bear in mind that 20 towers and defence gates, 12 churches, 3 monastery buildings and 8 large public buildings, dozens of historical granaries and industrial buildings were destroyed, burnt or seriously damaged. Among them were such unique structures as the Big Mill and the Crane, such rare fortification buildings as the Wisłoujście fortress and Stone Sluice and, finally, over a thousand burghers' houses.

In face of this great destruction, there was reason to ask: is it possible to reconstruct the city? Aside from the financial considerations, can artisans be found able to reconstruct what the best masters of various periods created here through the ages? It would not have been strange if a nation exhausted by war — a nation six million of whose citizens were killed and 38 per cent of whose national property was destroyed — had failed to undertake this extremely difficult task. However, the task was undertaken, almost immediately after the war ended. Of course, the first step was to secure everything that remained and to save it from further destruction. Later, the smaller damages were repaired and, only after the appropriate studies were completed and detailed documentation worked out, was it possible to begin the reconstruction work. "Reconstruction" is not the best word here because it suggests that the state that existed before the destruction was restored. It is true that in many cases

Abandoning the idea of reconstruction and eliminating the remnants of 19th-century buildings, Medieval defensive walls of the Main Town have been uncovered. A section of the Well Dungeon, a section of the wall and the Straw Dungeon; in the background — the Arsenal

this was the only aim but in many others "reconstruction" meant the re-establishment of the state that had existed, not before destruction, but earlier — before the deforming alterations. In both these cases it was often necessary to alter the interiors of the reconstructed building to fit their new functions. The general principle, without which no reconstruction could have taken place, was not to create dead museum exhibits but utilitarian buildings.

Of course, they had to be as useful as possible without distorting their character.

Work on most of the historical defence buildings — the towers and city gates — was an example of reconstruction in the exact meaning of the word. The following towers of the Main Town were rebuilt: Słomiana (Straw), Jacek (Hyacinthus), Łabędź (Swan), the tower of the Szeroka (Wide) Gate, Chlebnicka Gate and the White Tower in the Old Suburb. The nearby Pod Zrębem (Frame) and Stągwie (Milk-can) towers were also rebuilt as were the following gates: Upland, Lowland and Żuławska. The Golden Gate required thorough reconstruction, together with the neighbouring Court of St George's Fraternity. Also a few granaries on Granary Island, the granary at Szafarnia and the Royal Granary on Ołowianka were all rebuilt.

The reconstruction of most of the churches was of a similar character. That of St Mary's Church was one of the greatest works of this type and no doubt one of the greatest maintenance works in general. Its area equals almost half a hectare (over an acre) and its volume 155,000 cubic metres. This body of the church has three aisles and a similar transept, covered with separate roofs over each nave. The area of the roofs after unfolding is 8,000 square metres. This gives an idea of the extent of the task. The reconstruction of the roofs, of course in steel and concrete, was done in the years 1947—1948. The next stage was to rebuild the ceilings. The task was especially difficult for two reasons: because the naves are 28 metres high and because the geometrical design of the ceilings is extremely varied. The height of the naves called for gigantic scaffoldings, but this was avoided by hanging special platforms under the ceiling, from which the whole work was performed. The variety of the ceilings made it impossible to apply any pattern and each plane of the ceiling had to be reproduced individually. The decorative ceilings, up to 12 metres wide, were made "on the spot" on centerings situated under the ribs. But the greatest difficulty was to find craftsmen-bricklayers who knew how

The reconstructed St Mary's Church — surrounded by the houses on Mariacka Street still in ruins (1950)

The original Gothic character was restored to the reconstructed St Mary's Gate; the old House of the Natural Science Society, now lodging the Archaeological Museum, received the Renaissance finial of its turret

to do this work. After the reconstruction was completed one of the pillars began to crack. The situation was dangerous — the ceilings, and even other parts of the church, might collapse. But the catastrophe was averted by immediately propping up the endangered pillar and then reinforcing it with an iron concrete casing.

Rebuilding other churches — St Elizabeth's, St Joseph's and the Royal Chapel as well as St Catherine's and Holy Trinity which were not then com-

pleted, did not present such problems, although this task was not simple either. Even the churches that were not rebuilt but only preserved, required difficult work. In St John's Church, the foundations and the collapsing wall of the chancel had to be reinforced and the whole had to be roofed. In St Bartholomew's Church the tower's tendency to lean further and further from the vertical had to be stopped as it threatened the whole building.

The Gothic rectory of St Mary's Church was also

In these fragments of walls, one could scarcely recognize the mighty towers of the Medieval Crane

Today, however, its characteristic silhouette rises over the Motława as in the old days. On the left — reconstructed houses in Świętego Ducha Street

In order to save the original parts of walls in Artus Court, a complex operation was performed, of putting new pillars under the remnants of vaults, to replace the old ones consumed by fire

rebuilt, as were St Elizabeth's Hospital and the monastery next to St Joseph's Church, which once belonged to the Carmelites; the Pomeranian Museum that had its seat in the former Franciscan monastery; the Opacki Palace located in Oliwa park, which was to house the Archaeological Museum; the building of the Natural Science Society; and the Crane, which was adapted for the use of the Maritime Museum.

The reconstruction of the ceilings in Artus Court entailed building four new, slim, granite pillars. Three of them had to replace the old billars that were still standing but were cracked by fire. On them rested the remnants of the beautiful, starred ceiling with many ribs. In order to avoid demolishing the ceiling, great skill was employed; the remnants of the ceilings were supported by powerful props, the old pillars were removed and new ones placed under the ceilings. On them, and on the new fourth pillar, the whole ceiling could now rest and the destroyed parts were reproduced.

The reconstruction of the Golden House was very similar; part of the frontal wall was saved. This was supported by a wooden scaffolding, and it had to wait several years before it was possible to erect the whole building behind it. Only then could the missing parts of the façade be replaced and the whole structure renewed.

In the Main Town Hall a great hole in the wall was filled and the ceilings and roof rebuilt. But the technically most difficult part of the reconstruction was to rebuilt the slim, thirty-five metres high,

While the interior of Artus Court has not recovered its former rich furnishings, it again delights with the beauty of its architectural form

A piece of the front wall — that was all that remained of the Golden House in 1945

Today, rebuilt with loving care, the Golden House again adorns the Long Market as before

The slender spire on the tower of the Main Tower Hall rises over the reconstructed houses of the Long Market and Długa Street

The gilt statue of King Sigismund Augustus has returned to the top of the Town Hall tower (photo taken in the studio during trial mounting)

What remained of the Big Mill was hardly suggestive of its original clumsy form. In the background — the tower of St Catherine's Church

This quaint decorative pattern is actually the construction frame of the huge roof...

crown of the tower, its top reaching a height of 84 metres above the ground. It was made of a steel construction and the exterior was an exact reproduction of the historical form. Also the metal monument of King Sigismund Augustus, which ornamented the gable of the crown, was reconstructed, in conformity to iconographic sources and the preserved remnants of the original. Both this monument and the fragments of the ornaments of the crown were gilded, raising a technical problem: the electrolytic gilding commonly applied nowadays cannot be guaranteed to last. So the conservators recalled the old method which is based on covering copper foil with an amalgam-gold diassolved in mercury, the mercury later being steamed off by heating. The destroyed clock was replaced by an electric mechanism and the carillon by an electronic device with the melody "Rota" recorded by bells. An

appropriate carillon is to be remodelled. It took longest to reconstruct interiors. Rooms on the ground floor, with preserved Gothic details, and the Bench Room were completed and ready for use in 1966; the Summer Council Room (Red) and the rest of the rooms were completed in 1969.

The Corner Tower and the Straganiarska (Standkeepers'), Mariacka (St Mary's) and part of the Zielona (Green) Gate are examples of reconstruction where distortions have been removed. Defaced in preceding ages, they regained their Gothic or Renaissance character after they were rebuilt. Also St James' Church, rebuilt in 1815, returned to its former appearance and purpose.

Many monumental buildings were rebuilt and adapted to serve new functions. According to this principle a new Golden House was built, except for the front wall. Also the Small Arsenal was adjusted to serve as a shed for taxis and the Small Mill to be the seat of the Fishing Association. The small Hospital Church of the Holy Ghost that was included among the buildings belonging to a new school and some schoolrooms were placed here. The buildings of the former Municipal Manor at the Corner Tower were assigned to the press distribution agency; the second part is being rebuilt as a seat of the Pathfinders' Organization.

The beautifully reconstructed Big Mill is used for offices and a storehouse, though it could have been converted, for example, into a tourist hostel. The carefully rebuilt and splendid monument of the Gdańsk Renaissance, the Great Arsenal, is used by the Advanced School of Plastic Arts. Unfortunately for the school purposes it was necessary to divide it up by walls (luckily only provisional) into smaller rooms. Thus, the architectonic assets of the interiors of this monument were destroyed. However, these mistakes can be corrected in the future.

The reconstruction of the whole city complex of the Main Town was undoubtedly the greatest, unprecedented task in the rebuilding of monuments. Before it was destroyed, it consisted of 1,200 buildings, and in this number were many of the most valuable monuments of Gdańsk. The war turned it into a dead desert of ruins and rubble. The area of this part of the city, nearly 35 hectares, testify to the size of this task, for this is more than twice as big as the Old Town in Warsaw. After preliminary discussions and study and after a few buildings had been reconstructed by various investors, it was

...which restored the Big Mill to its original form. The partly reconstructed St Catherine's Church, on the other hand, is still waiting to get back its spire

Damaged outer walls are all that remained of Opberghen's masterpiece, the Great Arsenal

The reconstruction of vaults and roofs brought the Arsenal back to life, and the renovation of façades restored its former appearance. View from Piwna Street

Mariacka Street, the Main Town's finest little street, has also been reconstructed. In the background — a section of St Mary's Church

decided to rebuild the whole complex as a residential development with a comparatively large number of services. The Workers' Development Institution undertook this investment. Only the most valuable historical buildings like the churches, the Great Arsenal, the gates and towers were to be rebuilt by the Voivodship Conservation Agency or by those who were to use them.

On the basis of city planning and programme studies, it was decided that the Main Town can become a settlement for approximately 11,000 inhabitants. Thus, besides flats, two elementary schools, three nursery schools, two crèches, a dispensary, shops, restaurants and a cinema were planned.

Abandoning the idea of reconstruction of outbuildings and of some houses, the congestion of pre-war buildings has been radically relieved

The lace-like gables of period houses. The elimination of 19th-century malformities turned the Main Town into an architectural complex of unique merit

The Long Market has become Gdańsk's showpiece again. Gables of houses at No. 14, 15 and 16 in the Long Market

It was impossible to rebuild the Main Town exactly as it had been before it was destroyed. Buildings within this area that had been appropriate at first, over the ages and especially in the 19th century, had become ridiculous. On some of the lots the area free of building was only a few square metres and others were completely built up. Therefore, the principle was adopted to clear the housing blocks of outbuildings and other constructions that had been added in the 18th and 19th centuries. The decision to change the Main Town for residential purposes required other alterations as well, like not rebuilding some of the very narrow streets and reducing the depth of the lots that were sometimes over twenty metres deep in the buildings. It was also impossible to exactly reconstruct the interiors of the residential buildings; they had to be adapted to contemporary needs and residential norms.

Special care was given to reproducing the architectural and city planning character of the streets. Detailed historical studies were a basis for designing the reconstruction of façades. The team of workers from the History of Architecture Department of the Gdańsk Technical University directed by Professor Marian Osiński, rendered special service in this field. However, the principle of reconstructing

Another example of utilizing the preserved parts of the old stone-work: the upper part of portal of the house No. 82 in Świętego Ducha Street; the portal was built in 1605 and rebuilt around 1850

Transom window of the Rococo portal No. 5/6 in the Long Market — a stone-work and wood-carving detail reconstructed with great care

compromises that were not always the best. But to all these criticisms there is an answer: it would have been quite impossible to rebuild such a great historical complex if not for the decision to use it for residential purposes and for the fact that this task was undertaken by one, nationalized investor. Devastated monumental centres in other countries offer examples here.

To conclude, we should like to explain still another problem connected with the reconstruction of the Gdańsk monuments. I am told that a certain German, while not hiding his admiration for everything that had been done in Gdańsk, did say: "I only do not understand why you Poles rebuild so carefully all these monuments which are in fact German." A misunderstanding? Naturally, but worth explaining. First, let us recall that in the thousand years of Poland's history, for only 270 years, and that in four separate periods, did Gdańsk belong to a Teutonic state, whether Prussia or Germany. It is enough to compare the dates when individual buildings were erected with the historic periods to see that the great majority of these monuments were built or at least gained their final forms during the periods when Gdańsk belonged to Poland.

The builders of these structures came from various countries and the Gdańsk bourgeoisie, though often they were of German descent, they manifested their connections with Poland by their generous — probably more than in any other Polish city — ornamentation of the buildings with the Polish eagle the coat of arms and portraits of Polish kings. Therefore, the Gdańsk monuments are to a large extent documents of the Polish character of Gdańsk, and as such we have rebuilt them. If some other types have also been rebuilt then this is due to the fact that they are works of art, including historical items of architecture and thus the property of all mankind. Moreover, a criterion of culture is one's attitude towards all historical monuments. Are more reasons required?

the look of the whole city as it was in one chosen period was not applied but in each individual case the variant most valuable from the architectural point of view was chosen from among the few possible. Thus, the slogan "We shall rebuild Gdańsk more beautiful than ever" was more than a propaganda cliché. Today, when the reconstruction is coming to an end, one can see the result with one's own eyes and be convinced.

Of course, the principle of reconstruction thus understood can be attacked by purist conservators. There is also no doubt that introducing residential functions into a historical complex required certain

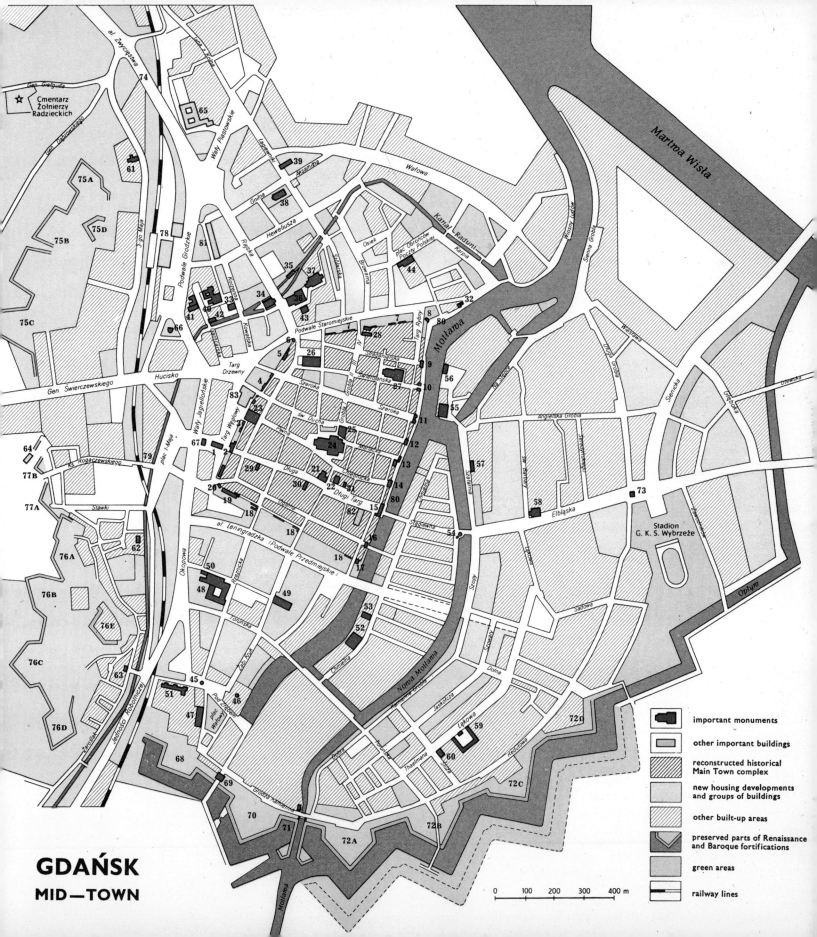

GDAŃSK
MID—TOWN

Martwa Wisła

Kanał Raduni

Mołtawa

Nowa Mołtawa

Stadion
G. K. S. Wybrzeże

important monuments

other important buildings

reconstructed historical Main Town complex

new housing developments and groups of buildings

other built-up areas

preserved parts of Renaissance and Baroque fortifications

green areas

railway lines

0   100   200   300   400 m

EXPLANATION OF NUMBERS

Monuments in the Main Town

1. Foregate of Długa Street (Prison Tower and Torture Chamber)
2. Golden Gate and Court of St George's Fraternity
3. Preserved section of Well Dungeon and defence wall, as well as Straw Dungeon
4. Section of defence wall and Lantern Tower and preserved tower of Wide Gate
5. "Na Zanurzu" (Beyond-the-wall) Tower
6. "Jacek" (Hiacynthus) Tower
7. Part of the northern line of the defence walls of the Main Town
8. Swan Tower
9. Standkeepers' Gate
10. St John's Gate
11. Crane Gate and port crane (now Maritime Museum)
12. Holy Ghost Gate
13. St Mary's Gate and House of the Natural Science Society now housing Archaeological Museum
14. Chlebnicka Gate
15. Green Gate
16. Cow Gate
17. Tower of the "Kotwiczników" Gate
18. Preserved sections of defence walls and Frog Gate
19. Brewer's and Schultz's Towers and southern part of municipal stables
20. Corner Tower
21. Main Town Hall
22. Artus Court and Neptune Fountain
23. Great Arsenal
24. St Mary's Church
25. Royal Chapel and presbytery of St Mary's Church
26. St Nicholas' Church
27. St John's Church
28. Hospital church and Holy Ghost Hospital
29. Uphagen House — 12 Długa Street
30. Lion's Castle — 35 Długa Street
31. Golden House — 41 Długi Targ Street

Monuments in the Old Town and Osiek

32. Parts of the wall and tower of the Teutonic Knights' Castle
33. Old Town Hall
34. Big Mill
35. Small Mill
36. St Catherine's Church
37. St Bridget's Church
38. St Bartholomew's Church
39. St James' Church
40. St Joseph's Church and monastery, formerly Carmelite
41. St Elizabeth's Church and monastery
42. Pelplin Abbots' House — 3 Elżbietańska Street
43. Preachers' House — 1-3 Katarzynki Street
44. Polish Post Office Building

Monuments in the Old Suburb

45. White Tower
46. "Pod zrębem" (Frame) Tower

47. Small Arsenal
48. Holy Trinity Church with St Anne's Chapel and former Franciscan monastery, now Pomeranian Museum
49. SS. Peter and Paul's Church
50. Gallery Building — 1 Holy Trinity Street
51. Polish Secondary School

Monuments on Granary Island, Ołowianka and Lower Town

52. Granaries: 59 Chmielna Street — "Under the Crown," 60, 61, 62 Chmielna Street
53. "Wisłoujście" Granary — 53 Chmielna Street
54. "Milk-can" Towers
55. "Oliwski" Granary — 11 Ołowianka Street
56. "Royal" Granary — 14 Ołowianka Street
57. "New Packing-room" Granary — 9 Szafarnia Street
58. St Barbara's Church
59. Former munitions factory — 35/38 Łąkowa Street
60. Neo-Classical House — 10 Śluza Street

Monuments in Podgórze

61. Corpus Christi Church
62. Mennonites' Church
63. Preserved part (tower) of Saviour Church at Zaroślak
64. Our Lord's Church
65. Building housing Polish railway main office between 1918—1939

Modern Fortifications

66. St Elizabeth's Bastion (preserved wall sections)
67. Upland Gate
68. St Gertrude's Bastion
69. Lowland Gate
70. Żubr (Bison) Rampart
71. Stone Sluice complex (sluice, defence structures and water mill)
72. Preserved bastions of Lower Town: A — Wolf Bastion, B — Jump Bastion, C — Teddy Bear Bastion, D — Rabbit Bastion
73. Żuławska Gate
74. Oliwska Gate — remained only a name of the place where the gate was located
75. Fortifications of Grodzisko Hill: A — Jerusalem Bastion, B — Marksmen's Bastion, C — Neubaur Bastion, D — Napoleon's Redoubt
76. Fortifications at Biskupia Górka: A — Vigilance Bastion, B — Ostroróg Bastion, C — Middle Bastion, D — Saviour's Bastion, E — Redoubt and former barracks
77. Preserved sections of the Siedlce Valley fortifications: A — Strakowski Bastion, B — preserved parts of Sand Bastion

Other Important Buildings

78. Main Railway Station
79. PKS — Long Distance Bus Station
80. Passenger Ships Port
81. "Orbis" Monopol Hotel
82. Jantar Hotel
83. Grand Theatre

GATE TO THE WORLD

Seas are the greatest communication routes in the world and ports are gates leading to these routes. Access to the sea itself cannot guarantee immediate participation in the great, world-wide trade but the possession of the appropriate gates, that is ports, does. This old truth lay at the basis of the development and wealth of many countries and today it remains equally timely.

If the ports are to fulfill their tasks, they must secure a safe entrance and stop-over for ships; they must be able to equip and repair them, organize the transloading and if necessary, store their goods. Each of these functions requires technical equipment: channels, docks, quays, cranes, storehouses, etc., adapted to the size of the ships expected and the type of transloading.

The history of navigation demonstrates a constant tendency to build larger and larger ships. This tendency, resulting from the increasing technical possibilities, is justified by economic considerations and became especially noticeable in the 19th and 20th centuries, in the period of the rapid development of technique. While, at the beginning of the present century, an average ship had a few thousand tons deadweight, at present it may have tens of thousands and there are more giants of hundreds of thousands of tons.

This increase in the size of ships requires the modernization and development of ports. The depth of port waters is an especially characteristic problem here: from about 1 metre in the early Middle Ages through a few metres in the 19th century to 15 and more metres necessary for the modern ocean-going giants. The problem of the width of the docks and channels, of the transloading equipment, the capacity of the storehouses, and finally the land communication junction serving the port — all these are important matters. The following comparison demonstrates how important the latter problem is: dozens of train wagons or more than a dozen lorries are necessary to transport the load of one large ocean-going vessel.

The ports that were not able to adapt their equipment to the growing tonnage of ships lost their significance, changed their character. Some of them became fishing ports and others were simply not

The old harbour of Gdańsk on the Motława was picturesque but not suited to the present needs. This is why it was decided in 1945 not to reconstruct it from the havoc of war

destruction. It was necessary to adapt them to the new political and economic conditions and to new, higher technical requirements.

When Poland regained her old territories on the Baltic Sea that had belonged to the Piast dynasty, it gained a third port besides Gdynia and Gdańsk — Szczecin, and also a few smaller ones. During the inter-war period over 70 per cent of Polish foreign trade was carried out by sea. The change in the structure of international relations reversed these proportions — at present two-thirds of the transactions are directed through the land. However, at the same time, the economic development and a con-

All efforts were concentrated instead on the recontruction and moderniaztion of the newer parts of the harbour situated on the broader and deeper waters of the Dead Vistual and the Port canal

used any more. One of the most characteristic phenomena connected with the fact that ports were adapting themselves to the increasing dimensions of ships is that they moved from deep inside bays and the mouths of rivers towards the sea, towards deeper and wider waters.

This phenomenon is also noticeable in Gdańsk. The small and quiet Motława located a few kilometres from the sea was an ideal port in the Middle Ages and it was still sufficient up to the 19th century. Bu then it became necessary to build a new part of the port near the sea that would be accessible to larger ships. This new investment was later developed along the line of the Dead Vistula. The old port on the Motława River, equipped with numerous granaries and storehouses was still used to serve smaller ships until it was destroyed in 1945.

To rebuild the ports, like the cities, could not mean merely reproducing what had existed before

The growing general-cargo transloadings called for the adaptation of the harbour to its new tasks. The reconstructed Marchlewski Quay

siderable increase in the industrialization of the country meant that the amount of goods passing through the Polish ports diminished during the first few years only; at present, it much exceeds the pre-war figure. The following figures demonstrate this: in 1938 a total of 19.3 million tons were transloaded in Polish ports, in 1949 — 16.9 million tons and in 1970 — 34.2 million tons.

The second factor that influences the work of the ports are the changes in the structure of Polish foreign trade, and in particularly the fact that the amount of raw material exported is diminishing in favour of industrial products. This causes the goods transloaded to be much more valuable but smaller and more difficult to handle. To adapt the ports to their new tasks required equipping them with new transloading devices, and increasing the space

covered by storehouses. This determined a wide programme of modernization and development, like the necessity of adapting new ports to serve ships of greater tonnage.

The Gdańsk port offers a typical example here. The transshipment of coal reached four million tons before the war; during the post-war period it diminished by half because it was taken over by Szczecin, a port that is much more conveniently located. The increasing transshipments of small goods were at first directed through the modern port in Gdynia that was best equipped for it. As a result, the transshipments in Gdańsk that amounted to 7.1 million tons before the war decreased to 5.2 million tons in 1955. The fact that the port of Gdańsk was not adapted to current economic needs and technical re-

During the transloading of Polish cars exported abroad, or of Czech cars in transit through Poland, a part of the harbour looks like a big parking area

Big cargo ships in the harbour of Gdańsk. can receive ships with
a capacity load of up to 35 thousand DWT

quirements, also had a great influence on the forms of its work.

It was necessary to begin work to radically change the technical conditions of the port. The modernization work that has already been completed made it possible to increase transshipments to 5.8 million tons in 1960 and 9.5 million tons in 1970. At present, the total transshipments in the Gdańsk-Gdynia port complex exceed 18 million tons annually. Yet the amount of transshipment does not fully reflect the changes coming to Gdańsk. The basic hydrotechnical works were finished in 1965 and their effect will be visible only in the years to come.

The greatest work was connected with making the port accessible for large ships. For this purpose, the water route leading from the ways, the entrance to the port and the Port Canal were widened and deepened, and a point of land that made manoeu-vering difficult was cut off at the Five Whistles' Turn. The widening of the Port Canal itself from 100 to 150 metres may give an idea of the dimension of this work. It required the removal of about a million cubic metres of earth and the building of about a kilometre and a half of new quays. Thus, it is now possible for ships with a displacement of up to 10 metres, over 200 metres long and of 35,000 tons to anchor at the port of Gdańsk. And what is more important — the work that has already been completed made it possible to further deepen the canal and make the port accessible for still larger ships.

The complete rebuilding of the region of the Vistula Station was another great investment in the Gdańsk port; it now bears the name of the Twentieth Anniversary Quay. The earth from widening the Port Canal was used to fill in the swamps, a new railway station, roads and storehouses were

Towering over the widened Port Canal and the entrance to the harbour is the monument erected in Westerplatte, dedicated to the memory of the Polish soldiers who died there in 1939, of the Polish seamen who died in the Second World War, and of the soldiers who fell in the struggle for the liberation of the coast in 1945

built, the quays were redesigned and equipped with new cranes. After the work is completed, this part of the port will be capable of transloading half a million tons of small goods annually.

At the Pięć Gwizdków Turning a new embarkment Obrońców Poczty Polskiej (Defenders of the Post Office), has been built specially for the reloading of exported sulphur.

Besides the changes mentioned above, other work is being conducted, connected with modernizing Oliwa Quay, with the thorough rebuilding of its background and with equipping the new Westerplatte Quay — both adjoining the Port Canal. Other work includes deepening the docks, building storehouses, modernizing the wooden port and equipping the port with cranes and other devices. Also, a new Harbour Master's Office, a base for equipment, and social buildings are being established.

As a result of the above mentioned work, the port is modern and is continually improved; it has at its disposal over eight kilometres of transloading quays, the total length of which equals 27.8 kilometres. The area covered by storehouses which in June, 1946, was 3,000 square metres, is now, not counting the storage and refrigerating buildings, nearing the 100,000 square metres mark. The transloading equipment includes approximately 90 immobile, about 30 mobile and 3 floating cranes and special equipment for transloading coal, grain and liquid fuels. Within the great area of the Gdańsk port, with its 10 square kilometres, it is difficult today to find a place not covered by an investment plan. The more than a thousand million złotys invested during the twenty years since the war in reconstruction, development and modernization of the port of Gdańsk has determinend the path of its transformation — from the historic Crane and the old granaries on the Motława to modern cranes and storehouses on the deep quays, to the widened Port Canal and entrance to the port. The Polish gate to the world has been opened wider.

INDUSTRY-NOT ONLY SHIPBUILDING

Gańsk is a highly industrialized city — of the 172,400 inhabitants employed in the national economy, over 66.5 thousand work in industrial plants. When these people are mentioned, usually the word "shipyards" is used. But it is not exactly accurate to identify Gdańsk industry with shipyards only, but on the other hand, one must admit that there are reasons justifying this idea.

The shipyard cranes that tower over the city and the bodies of ships that grow on slips are both very characteristic and suggestive elements in the city landscape. This is the industry that is most noticeable.

And this industry is very important. The position held by the shipyards results from the role that is now played by the shipbuilding industry in the country's economy. Although shipbuilding has very old traditions in Poland, it began to develop as a modern industry, very slowly at first, in the 1930's. The Nazi invasion destroyed even this modest achievement. After the Second World War Poland took over the shipyards that were then ruined and devastated. In 1948, without the experts and often without appropriate equipment, building was begun on the first ships — steam-driven ore and coal carriers, with a carrying capacity of 2,540 tons. The first of these ships, *Sołdek*, was handed over for use towards the end of 1949. Poland was placed on the list of producers of ocean-going vessels, of course in the last place. After 16 years the Polish shipbuilding industry found itself in the tenth position in the world with the production of 480,000 tons DWT (1968), outdistancing even Holland, Denmark and the United States. In export production Poland holds an even higher position, being in seventh place, while in building fishing vessels the first.

This dynamic and even astonishing development of the shipbuilding industry in Poland was caused both by the country's needs and by the large number of foreign orders, especially from the Soviet Union. In 1950—1969 the Polish merchant marine was increased from 52 to 250 ships and its carrying capacity increased almost eight-fold, reaching 1,843,000 tons deadweight. It serves now over 50 per cent of the Polish overseas trade. Therefore, its further development is planned and in the near future it will reach about two million tons and after some years between four and five million.

The development of the fishing fleet presents a similar picture. In order to increase the amount of fish consumption in Poland, which was too low, the range of fishing had to be increased. Since the Baltic fishing grounds are not very productive, only the richer grounds of the North Sea and the Atlantic Ocean could offer an increase in the fishing take. However, in order to fish on the distant fishing grounds of Norway, Newfoundland and Africa,

The Lenin Shipyard in Gdańsk ranks among the world's biggest shipbuilding plants

A fishing base-ship, with a capacity of 10 thousand DWT, built at the Gdańsk Shipyard to the order of a Soviet shipping company

a special fishing fleet consisting of refrigerator-trawler, factory-trawler and base ships for smaller units was required. These needs, too, had to be fulfilled by the shipbuilding industry. Today, all the types of fishing ships that we need are built in our own shipyards and it is worth stressing that such ships as trawler-factories or fishing bases, which are among the most complicated units, are built only in a few countries in the world.

Thanks to modern construction methods and to the quality of production, the Polish shipbuilding industry receives orders from the four corners of the world. Ships built in Poland sail under the flags of over a dozen countries. Besides our most important customer, the Soviet Union, they also include such distant and exotic countries as the Chinese People's Republic, Indonesia, India and Pakistan, the United Arab Republic, Libya and Kuwait, Brazil and Cuba and also European countries like Czechoslovakia, Albania and Switzerland and even countries with a developed shipbuilding industry like Great Britain, France and Norway.

The Gdańsk Shipyard was the first to begin production after the war. It was here that *Sołdek* and a whole series of ore and coal carriers were built and later various mass-produced and small goods carriers, tankers and various ships for ocean fishing. Altogether in the years 1948—1970, the Gdańsk Shipyard built a powerful fleet consisting of 551 ships of over twenty different types, with carrying capacity 2.7 million tons. At present, the Gdańsk Shipyard, which was named after Lenin in 1967, is

among the best shipyards in the world. It builds about thirty ships every year. Approximately 90 per cent of this production is exported. The ships that are built here, all of them motorships designed by Polish specialists, give excellent service and are beautiful as well. The shipyard also builds elementary equipment such as great ship boilers and internal-combustion engines that develop several thousand horsepower. This industry employs 18,000 workers. As a basis of comparison, it is worth mentioning that in tonnage alone, not counting the difference in the value of the ships, the present

The spectacular moment of "sideways" launching of a modern trawler-factory

production is ten times the average inter-war annual production of both shipyards which formed the basis of the present shipyard.

Four other shipyards also belong to the shipbuilding industry in Gdańsk. The Gdańsk Repairing Shipyard which employs over five thousand people, repairs between one and two hundred ships a year and also builds floating docks. The two remaining shipyards: the Northern and Vistula (formerly the Gdańsk River Shipyard) produce smaller ocean-going and inland units. The Vistula Shipyard specializes in building ships of plastic and light aluminium ores (hydronalium). Thanks to these modern production methods, it won the competition announced by FAO, the International Food and Agricultural Organization, and built a series of hydrographic ships for Pakistan. It was also here that the first Polish hydroplane was built.

The transportation industry holds a dominant position in Gdańsk. Besides the shipyards it consists of a "Hydroster" plant which produces steering, hydraulic and other ship mechanisms; it also includes a large railway workshop, a factory for car parts and a few smaller factories.

All these plants, except for one that was built up entirely after the war, are old plants rebuilt after the devastations of war, when they were modernized and often much enlarged.

The food industry occupies second place from the point of view of the number of employees. It includes fats, meat, fish, fruit and vegetable factories, and also the production of beer, sweets, chocolate and nutriments. In this field, the old, rebuilt but often modernized and extended factories form the majority. Only the dairy industry and the great refrigerated storehouse are completely new.

Group of floating docks of the Gdańsk Repairing Shipyard. In the dock on the right — the training frigate of the Polish Merchant Marine *Dar Pomorza*

To the order of the FAO. Wisła Shipyard built a series of hydrographic ships of plastic for Pakistan

Poland's first hydrofoil, designed by experts from the Gdańsk Technical University and built by the Wisła Shipyard, mainly from light aluminium alloys

The Gdańsk electric engineering industry holds third place. The most important plants are Elmor, the Gdańsk radio plant, and the Electric Assembling Plant. The last named produces motors, electrical equipment for ships, radio equipment and television sets and finally electric power equipment for industrial plants, including that for complete plants of various types that Poland exports to other countries.

The machine and metal construction industries play an important part, although they are only in fourth place as to the number of employees. The Precision Machine Plant is one of the most interesting in this field; it produces ship compasses, very sensitive analytical scales, aqualungs, other equipment and precision instruments. This plant exports over 40 per cent of its production to dozens of countries all over the world. Other Gdańsk plants produce machines and equipment for treating wood, building machines: vibrohammers, vibrating ground condensers, etc. and also equipment for the fodder industry and various metal constructions. Some of the plants of this group are housed in new buildings (e.g., the Precision Engineering Plant), others are waiting for the appropriate rooms and buildings to be completed.

The yacht shipyard and the furniture factory are the most important plants in the wood industry and their production is mainly for export. The yacht shipyard which lies on the Dead Vistula is a modern plant that was built from scratch.

The chemical industry, which is represented by

The new building of the Elmor plant, producer of nautical electrical equipment

Interior of the Gdańsk Elektromontaż plant which exports power equipment to a large number of countries

Precision Machine Plant in Gdańsk-Oliwa

19 plants, came low on the list in Gdańsk because these were small plants. From among them one should mention the new industry manufacturing technical gases and the paint and lacquer factory which is housed in old buildings, but produces special ship paints of a high quality. The third more important plant is the sulphuric acid factory which is being absorbed by a large phosphoric fertilizer plant that is now being built. A plant is being set up that costs 1,200 million zlotys, which will produce 300,000 tons of triple-strength superphosphate annually. Partly, it will utilize raw materials which will be imported by sea and this is why it is located in Gdańsk, with its own transloading quays, accessible to large ocean-going vessels. When this plant is built it will fundamentally change the position of the chemical industry in the city and even in Gdańsk Voivodship; it will introduce a new large chemical industry to Gdańsk.

From among the plants that belong to other branches of industry, the following are worth mentioning as the most important or the most characteristic: the fur and haberdashery plants and a works making laboratory glass and Christmas tree ornaments, mainly for export. Only this last plant was built from the beginning; the rest are housed in rebuilt or more or less expanded buildings.

Altogether, Gdańsk industry consists of 349 plants, of which 272 are small and employ less than 100 people, 69 are medium and employ from 100 to 1,000 people and only 8 are large and employ over 1,000. However, these last employ over 53 per cent of all those employed in Gdańsk industry. The spatial location of the plants is also characteristic:

The big Phosphate Plant is still under construction but some departments are already working

districts located in the appropriate places and well organized. In fact, most of the new plants were built in such areas. As a result, three distinct new industrial-storage areas developed: the Wrzeszcz-Oliwa belt, the region of Litewska Street and the Młyniska district that lies between Wrzeszcz and Nowy Port. Thus, an important step was taken in the direction of the proper spatial structure of the city, towards reducing difficulties and creating advantageous conditions for industrial communication and technique. Unfortunately, it was not possible to fully realize this good principle because also some badly located plants were rebuilt out of economic necessity. Especially undesirable were those instances in which it was impossible to build isolated zones around the plants already existing or those that were being rebuilt.

Assembly line in the TV-set assembling department of the Gdańsk Radio Works

44 per cent of them, but employing less than 20 per cent of the staff, are located in Wrzeszcz together with Oliwa; the smallest number, only 56 plants (16 per cent) but employing 56 per cent of the staff are located in the port district.

It is difficult to characterize the town-planning and architectural aspect of Gdańsk industry because it is so varied. The former industrial plants that date back to the 19th and the early 20th century were dispersed among residential and public utility buildings. This became very troublesome and even harmful to the inhabitants and caused many problems for city traffic. The direction of development set by the city planners was to create industrial

From the architectural point of view the industrial plants in Gdańsk make extremely varied impressions. The old plants are usually of the type that was characteristic of the end of the 19th century. The new plants on the whole make a better impression, though the buildings erected after 1955 represent more interesting construction and architectural designs. The reason for this is easy to understand — during the first years after the war the necessity to begin production was predominant and at the same time, there was difficulty with materials and building.

One of the newly-built warehouses. Its shape and architectonic form were so designed as to match the old buildings on Granary Island

Gdańsk Industry 1968		
Branch of Industry	Number of Plants	Number of Employees
Producing electric and thermal energy	4	946
Fuel Industry	2	665
Machine and Metal Construction Industry	18	2,960
Electrical Engineering Industry	17	4,464
Means of Transportation Industry	24	33,372
Metal Industry	42	2,416
Chemical Industry	12	2,101
Rubber Industry	2	374
Building Materials Industry	6	734
Glass Industry	16	388
Wood Industry	23	2,842
Paper Industry	11	831
Polygraphical Industry	6	553
Textile Industry	7	1,196
Clothing Industry	29	1,002
Leather and Footwear Industry	45	1,367
Food Industry	73	6,498
Others	12	532

Storage is a separate field of the economy but it is connected with industry. Gdańsk did not have modern means of storing goods suitable for contemporary requirements and what did exist was devastated by the war. Immediate needs and the restricted investments meant that buildings which could be used for storing purposes were rebuilt or altered and provisional buildings were set up. During the last few years several new warehouses have either been built or are planned to satisfy the increasing needs. However, the need in this field is much greater.

The reconstruction of a few old granaries on Granary Island for storing purposes are desirable from the architectonic point of view. The multi-storey warehouse of the Pharmacy Administration built next-door is also worth mentioning. It is a good example of adapting a modern building to its historical surroundings. Comparing it with the granary that was built between the world wars at 26 Chmielna Street (opposite St Mary's Gate) offers a model of an architectural and cultural attitude towards monuments.

ADMINISTRATION, SCIENTIFIC AND CULTURAL CENTRE

As the capital of the voivodship, Gdańsk is the seat of the administrative and economic administration of Gdańsk Voivodship. This voivodship is one of the smallest in the country — it covers an area of 10,984 square kilometres and is 15th, that is third from the last, as to size. However, it has a dense population: 132 inhabitants per square kilometre, while the country's average is 105. As a result, Gdańsk Voivodship with its 1,462,000 inhabitants holds eleventh place from the point of view of the number of inhabitants. As respects urbanization, it holds an even higher place: it has 1,014,000 inhabitants living in the cities, that is 69.4 per cent, which places it second in the country — after Katowice Voivodship, which covers the most industrialized regions of the country — the Upper Silesian Industrial Basin.

Gdańsk Voivodship also plays an important role in the country's economy. As respects the value of industrial production it is in eighth place. It plays an even more important role in the sea economy, accounting for over two-thirds of the ship production, 56 per cent of port transloadings and over 50 per cent of unloading sea fish.

The functions of a voivodship capital and the economic meaning of this area determine the role of Gdańsk as an administrative centre. Thus, Gdańsk is the seat of the Voivodship National Council and its bodies, the voivodship financial and insurance agencies, the administration of justice, the voivodship administrations and executives of associations, organizations and enterprises. In some fields of administration, the range of Gdańsk's influence goes beyond the borders of the voivodship and covers either the whole of the seashore or the neigbouring voivodships, for Gdańsk is one of the few cities in Poland whose influence covers more than one region. The lower levels of administration cover functions connected with the city itself: the Municipal and District National Councils and their bodies, institutions, organizations, managements of enterprises etc.

Altogether over 5,000 people are employed in public administration, financial and insurance institutions and in the administration of justice in Gdańsk. This number does not include those employed in the administration of the economy.

The buildings occupied by the Gdańsk offices and

The new meeting room of the Voivodship National Council

The designing offices that were formally included in other branches of the national economy are closely connected with Gdańsk as a management and service centre. There are 27 of them in Gdańsk, of which 12 are connected with the construction and 4 with the shipbuilding industry. One should mention here the most important designing offices: of General Building, Industrial Building, Maritime Building, Communal Building and Rural Building, as well as two offices for communication designing. "Prozamet," the Enterprise for Designing and Building Metallurgical and Electric Engineering Industrial

Office building of the Centromor Company for Foreign Trade. In the back — the buildings of the former Town Court at the exit of Ogarna Street; in the background — the tower of the Main Town Hall

institutions vary in architecture. The highest authority — the Presidium of the Voivodship National Council is located in an old building that has only been partially reconstructed. The Presidium of the Municipal National Council is located in a new building built in 1948—1950. Of the three District National Councils one is located in an old building and the other two in new ones which, however, were built to serve other purposes and are ill-adapted to the requirements of the present users. Financial institutions and the administration of justice are placed in buildings dating back to the end of the 19th or the beginning of the 20th century. Only the branches of the Polish National Bank received new offices. The administration of the economy, that is, various trade centres, and the administration of enterprises, make use of both partly reconstructed old buildings and new ones built after 1945. The new buildings were mainly erected in the mid-town district and in Wrzeszcz.

The General Building Designing Office lodged next to the historical House of the Pelplin Abbots

building Industry that is now being erected. This building consists of a lower part where the laboratories are located and a 17-storey office part that is original in its construction. The whole building has much glass in the exterior walls and is supported by two columns that are hidden inside. Also the system of building was original: first, the two columns were set up by the gliding method and then each ceiling was covered with concrete from a matrix that was gradually lowered, so that the building, to the amazement of observers, "grew" from its roof down.

The Communal Building Designing Office has erected its office building in Wrzeszcz

Plants, is of a special character. This is a designing office and at the same time an enterprise that undertakes the building of industrial plants of its own design; it also has at its disposal plants that produce some of the equipment for the new factories. Most of "Prozamet's" activity is meant for export. For example, it has built shipyards in Indonesia, Cuba and Iceland. The Main Constructional-Research Centre of the Shipbuilding Industry is another designing office of a special character.

Most of the designing offices are located in new buildings. The most magnificent seats were set up by the General Building Designing Office and "Prozamet" in the mid-town, the Communal Building Designing Office and the communications designing offices in Wrzeszcz. But they are all outdistanced both in size and modernity by the building of the Main Constructional-Research Centre of the Ship-

Also erected in Wrzeszcz is the office building of two transportation designing bureaux. On the right — the administration building of the dairy plant

This is what the seat of the Main Constructional-Research Centre of the Shipbuilding Industry will look like when its construction is completed

The strong scientific centre existing in Gdańsk has an important meaning for the economic and social development of the city and the region. It is formed by 6 institutions of higher learning, 5 institutes and 26 regional scientific-research centres and a few other institutions of a scientific type. About 12,000 students take regular courses at Gdańsk institutions of higher learning and almost 5,000 take evening and extra-mural courses. The number of research and teaching staff exceeds 2,000 of whom 120 are full or associate professors and over 220 *docents,* or approximately assistant professors. It is worthwhile to compare these data with the numbers that illustrate the state of higher learning in Gdańsk before 1939: two institutions of higher learning with a total of 1,300 to 1,500 students and 94 scientific workers on the staff.

The Gdańsk Technical University is the largest of the institutions of higher learning in the city, attended by almost half the students and employing over 45 per cent of the scientific staff. The Gdańsk Technical University has 9 departments which include the only Shipbuilding Department in Poland, which has trained almost all the specialists working in the Polish shipbuilding industry. The former buildings, rebuilt from ruins, were not sufficient for an institution of higher learning that now has three times as many students as before the war. Therefore, new buildings were set up for the following departments: Hydroconstruction, Shipbuilding and Electronics. The Technical University has already overflowed its former area and now the large blocks of its new buildings begin to dominate the whole complex of university buildings.

The second largest school is the Medical Academy which has approximately 2,580 students in all its departments and 625 scientific workers. This school

The largest group of student's hostels of the Gdańsk Technical University has been built in Wyspiańskiego Street in Wrzeszcz

did not have appropriate buildings since it had not existed as an institution of higher learning before 1945. The medical and stomatological departments were located in various renovated buildings at the clinic hospital, some even newly built. The Pharmacy Department, on the other hand, was located in a former school building. Now, the Pharmacy building is being extended and at the same time a complex of buildings for the the theoretical section of the Medical Department are being constructed.

The Advanced School of Pedagogy was at first located in an old building which soon ceased to be adequate. The situation was temporarily improved by altering and constructing provisional buildings, but since the number of students was 30 times as great as before the war and the school was to be enlarged, it was decided to build a new complex of buildings on another, larger area.

The Advanced State School of Plastic Arts which was organized in Sopot after the war was transferred in the 1950's to Gdańsk, where the higher storeys of the reconstructed Arsenal were provisionally adapted for its needs. Later a new wing of the building was constructed on a neighbouring area

A new wing of the Pharmacy Department of the Medical Academy

The Gdańsk Library of the Polish Academy of Sciences boasts a large number of valuable old prints

The documents preserved in the collection acquaint us with the history of the city and with living conditions in the past centuries; they also frequently bear witness to the Polish character of Gdańsk. An ordinance of the Town Council issued in Polish in 1738

where former tenement houses were destroyed during the war; its architecture is original but unfortunately not in harmony with the historic surroundings. As an academy of one of the arts, it is of course much smaller than the former ones; it has approximately 280 students and 60 on the art staff.

The last of the Gdańsk institutions, one that has existed for only a few years, was also transferred here from Sopot; it is the Academy of Music. The new building, in the mid-town, also houses an elementary and secondary music school and is thus a real "combine" of musical schools.

The students' hostels are closely connected with higher education. There are 19 of them in Gdańsk with over 5,000 beds, accomodating nearly half of the students of Gdańsk. Most of them are concentrated in three groups: at Hibnera and Wyspiańskiego streets (the Technical University's hostels) and at Dębowa Street (the Medical Academy's hostels). This latter group, which was designed and built as a unit, is most effective looking.

The centres of the Polish Academy of Sciences should be mentioned first among scientific institutions. They are the Institute of Hydroconstruction and the Institute of Flow Machines. The first conducts research on ocean and inland water construction, ground and foundation mechanics. The second works on problems that lie at the basis of the development of the Polish turbine industry. The Archaeological Laboratory of the Archaeology Research Centre of Greater Poland and Pomerania and the Gdańsk Laboratory of the Research Centre of the History of Pomerania, are much smaller institutions of the Polish Academy of Sciences, but they also have important scientific tasks.

The next group consists of scientific centres that

The former Franciscan monastery, rebuilt from war destruction, houses the Pomeranian Museum. Among its possessions is a valuable collection of products of Gdańsk's artistic handicraft

Bearing witness to the Gdańsk master's skill is the gilded silver "boatmen's cup" adorned with effigies of Polish kings, a work of Jan Jode from the beginning of the 18th century

are mainly connected with the maritime economy. The Maritime Institute is the largest of them; it works on technical and economic problems of the development and use of ports and the merchant marine. The Maritime Medical Institute is extremely important to the work of our sailors, fishermen and all people of the sea, as well as to Polish specialists who travel to tropical countries. The Maritime Electrical Engineering Section of the Electrical Engineering Institute works exclusively on technical problems. The Baltic Institute is of a different character and is interested in the history, the economic and social problems of the countries that lie on the Baltic Sea.

Other Gdańsk research centres study the problems of building, agriculture, organization of industry, automatics, communication, hydro-economy, inland fishing and forestry.

The Voivodship State Archives and the centres that conduct dual activity — scientific and cultural — are of a different character than those previously mentioned. Among them are the Gdańsk Library of the Polish Academy of Science and the Pomeranian, Archaeological and Maritime museums. Fortunately the building of the Library of the Polish Academy of Sciences was not seriously damaged, the State Archives and the Pomeranian Museum were rebuilt, the Archaeological Museum was set up in the reconstructed Natural Science Society building and the Maritime Museum received the Crane building, reconstructed and adapted to its needs. The Ethnographical Department of the Pomeranian Museum was located in the rebuilt Abbots' Palace in Oliwa. The Gdańsk Scientific Society also conducts both research and cultural activity on the old Gdańsk traditions and continues the work of the Friends of Science and Culture Society that was founded in 1922.

One of the exhibition rooms of the Archaeological Museum with reconstructed Early Medieval boats

The modern building of the *Wybrzeże* (Coast) Theatre in the Coal Market

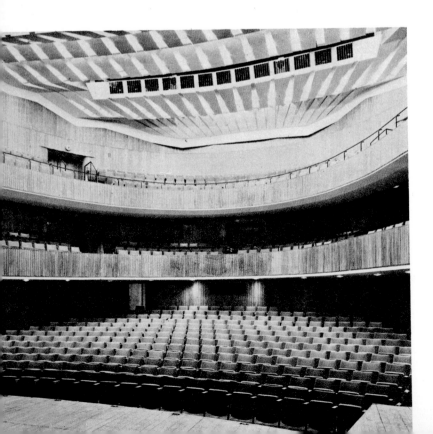

The opera, philharmonic, two theatres: dramatic and puppet, a radio and television transmitting centre, a socio-cultural monthly *Litery* (Letters) — these are the main institutions of the voivodship's cultural life; in some instances their influence reaches the whole country. To this should be added the museums already mentioned, as well as the activity of the Gdańsk Friends of Culture Society, artistic associations and societies, as well as numerous clubs among which the very active "Żak" student club deserves first mention.

Gdańsk's material base for its cultural life — the buildings that serve it — does not correspond to its

The house has 710 seats

development. The dramatic theatre is an exception since not long ago it has received a wonderful seat in a reconstructed, or rather new building in its old place on the Coal Market. This building covers approximately 36,000 cubic metres and, together with the neighbouring buildings which form its background, over 54,000 cubic metres. It has 710 seats, a revolving stage and extremely modern technical equipment. It assures excellent conditions both for the spectators and the actors. Both from outside and inside, the theatre has been given effective and modern architectonic forms which bravely or, as some critics say — too bravely, contrast with the neighbouring monuments.

The Opera and Philharmonic are housed in a building that was rebuilt from a former sports hall, the Miniature Theatre and most of the remaining cultural institutions received places that were either reconstructed or adapted; they basicaly fulfill their functions but are not worthy of special attention. Exceptions are: the Voivodship House of Folk Art that has its seat in the Old Town Town Hall and the Society of Polish Architects that is located in the reconstructed seat of St George's Fraternity and the neighbouring Golden Gate.

Gdańsk and Gdańsk Voivodship are among the areas of Poland with the highest number of radio and television owners. Since 1945, when the first, primitive radio station started operating in the buildings of the old fort, much has changed for the better. For instance, a new radio and television transmitting centre, much stronger than the first,

The Press House in the Timber Market. On the lawn is a statue of King John III Sobieski

has been built in Chwaszczyn. The studios are still housed in a few altered buildings that are neither sufficient nor appropriate. The problem of building the required radio and television centre is still awaiting a solution.

While discussing the role of Gdańsk as a cultural centre, one should not forget about the daily press. It is represented in Gdańsk by three dailies. Their editorial boards are located in the Press House that was built in the Timber Market in the 1950's.

While evaluating the situation in Gdańsk as concerns cultural buildings and equipment in general, one should remember the neglect before the war, the devastations of the war and the difficulties in rebuilding the whole country after the war. The situation of Gdańsk is not worse, but sometimes even better than in many cities of richer countries that were not destroyed. However, it does not compare favourably with other Polish cities and existing disproportions must be removed.

TOURISM AND TOURISTS

For a long time now, it has been the custom to mark the more interesting places with stars in tourist guides and folders. The stars in guide books play an important role in the tourist movement; like a magnet they draw to certain towns throngs of people searching for beautiful landscapes, interesting buildings or places famous for historical events.

If one should sum up all the stars used in guide books to mark its monuments and places interesting from the tourist point of view, Gdańsk would have several dozen of them and over ten places marked with more than one star.

A conservation classification gives us much more detailed and more meaningful information about the historical value of Gdańsk. In Gdańsk there are 665 places that are officially acknowledged as monuments and given a conservator's care. Of this number, three buildings belong to the highest, "zero" group, 33 to group 1, 117 to group 2 and 191 to group 3. The urban complex of the Main Town, St Mary's Church with its immediate surroundings and the Great Arsenal belong to group 0, the highest group. Among the places in group 1 are: the urban complex of the old port on the Motława, the Crane, Golden, Upland, Green and Lowland gates, the Prison Tower and the Torture Chamber, the seat of St George's Fraternity, the Hiacynthus Tower, St Catherine's, St Nicholas', St John's and the Holy Trinity churches together with the former Franciscan Monastery and its St Anne's Chapel, the Royal Chapel, the Wisłoujście Fortress, the Lower Town's and St Gertrude's bastions, the Main Town Hall, the Assessor's House, Artus Court and Neptune Fountain, the Golden House, Uphagen House, the Lion Castle, the Pelplin Abbots' House, the Arcade House in Lipce, the cathedral and monastery complex left by the Cistercian monks in Oliwa and places devoted to special national memory: Westerplatte and the building of the former Polish Post Office in the Free City of Gdańsk.

The second group covers the urban complexes of the Coal Market and Granary Island, preserved sections of the defence walls of the Main Town, Milk-can and Żuławska Gate, the Small Arsenal and Old Town, Town Hall, 6 churches, 47 burghers' houses and 8 granaries, a few old industrial build-

The splendid historical monuments raised from ruins are Gdańsk's main tourist attraction. Part of the Main Town on the Motława; in the background: left — St Mary's Church, right — the Crane

ings (mills, a water smithery), courts, institutions and hospitals, certain parts of modern fortifications and also engineering constructions — the Radunia Canal, and the Stone Sluice.

The monuments that belong to the remaining groups are too many even to list easily. As one can see, a tourist cannot complain of a lack of places of interest in Gdańsk.

The tourist attractions of Gdańsk do not end with the monuments. The port is interesting, especially to a newcomer who is not acquainted with the mar-

Apart from the centre of the city, the most important group of historical monuments is to be found in Oliwa. It consists of the Cathedral (former Cistercian church), the abbots' palace and the adjacent park. The photo shows the façade of the Cathedral

itime economy; here are ships from many countries of the world, strange crews and goods, cranes and transshipment, storehouses and the traffic on the canal. Some plants are also a great attraction, and especially the Gdańsk Shipyard. Even seen only from the deck of a small ship it impresses one by the number and modernity of the ships that are being built there, and taking part in the docking of a huge ocean liner may be a thrilling experience.

For those who are interested in neither the port nor industry, Gdańsk has three museums with very interesting collections and temporary exhibitions: it also has two theatres, an opera and philharmonic, as well as exhibitions and festivals which are held during the annual Days of Gdańsk and Days of the Sea. The International Song Festival in Sopot is also a tourist attraction, as are some of the sport competitions, as for example the World Fencing Championships that were held here in 1963 or the World Sailing Championships in the Finn Class which were held in Gdynia in 1965.

Tourists who want to rest can, of course, find better conditions for doing so in the small towns on the coast, but in Gdańsk itself there also are sandy beaches with a park or forest behind them and on the western edge of the city there are vast forests with various types of trees; they cover picturesquely the rolling areas of the moraine upland.

The cruises of excursion ships around Gdańsk Bay, between Gdańsk, Sopot and Gdynia, to the ports of the Hel Peninsula, or along inland routes, offer many experiences and beautiful views, as well as an opportunity to rest.

One cannot omit the role of Gdańsk as a starting point for various interesting trips to near and more distant regions. The whole Gdańsk Coast should be mentioned among the places worth visiting: from Łeba with its shifting sand dunes in the west to Piaski, hidden among the forests of the Vistula strip in the east. As examples we may mention here Jastrzębia Góra, beautifully located on the western part of the coast, on a high, cliff shore, the summer resorts Jastarnia and Jurata and the fishing village

A detail of the interior of the Cathedral, an interesting document of its Cistercian past: the stairs connecting the friars' dormitory with the transept of the church

of Hel that all lie on the Hel Peninsula, also of the oldest towns in Pomerania, Puck, that lies on Puck Bay. There are many bathing resorts to the east of Gdańsk: Sobieszewo, Mikoszewo, Jantar, Stegna, Sztutowo, Kąty Rybackie and Krynica Morska. The Nazi concentration camp of Stutthof, where there is now a museum, was near Sztutowo. Towards the south-west from Gdańsk there is a vast land of forests and lakes — the Kashubian Lakeland. This

is a region that is extremely interesting to tourists, because of both its landscapes and folklore. The group of Radunia lakes and the neighbouring Wieżyca, the highest point in northern Poland (329 metres above sea level) and also the great complex of Wdzydze Lake, called the Kashubian Sea, are most interesting, especially for their beautiful landscapes.

The surroundings of Gdańsk are also rich in architectural monuments. Especially interesting are the monastery complexes in Pelplin, Żarnowiec and Żukow, which is beautifully located above the Radunia Valley, and some sections of the small town of Kartuzy, which is the capital of the county, and relics of the former Żuławy architecture.

Somewhat further, but still within reasonable distance for an excursion by car, is Malbork, with its great castle of the Teutonic Knights, which now houses a museum and is one of the largest Medieval fortresses in Europe. Sometimes plays or historical performances are staged in the castle yard; within this scenery they make a greater impression on the spectators than against the background of ordinary theatrical settings.

Although it lies 95 kilometres from Gdańsk, Frombork is also worth visiting, the place where the great astronomer, Nicolaus Copernicus, spent over thirty years of his life, where he conducted his observations and worked on his great book. The fortified monastery complex that lies on a hill consists of a 14th century church, one of the most beautiful sacral monuments of northern Poland, Copernicus's tower-observatory and a modest museum.

It is not surprising that Gdańsk, which is a great tourist attraction and which has so many interesting places and areas nearby, draws many tourists. This movement is constantly increasing. In 1960

The Westerpaltte monument — on the spot where the first shots of the Second World War were fired and where the first casualties occurred — is the object of many excursions

Pleasure boats of the "white fleet" at the Long Pier on the Motława. On the left — the Chlebnicka Gate, the Archaeological Museum, Mariacka (St Mary's) Gate and the Crane

The sheltered waters of Gdańsk Bay provide convenient sailing conditions

approximately 300,000 tourists visited Gdańsk and at present as many as 2 million a year. Of course, most of them were from other parts of the country, but recently there have been more and more tourists from abroad coming to visit the city. Many of them come by tourist ships.

Tourism does not only mean tourist attractions and the tourists that come to see them; it also means various facilities to serve them. From this point of view, the situation in Gdańsk is not as good. There are only three hotels here and they can house but a small fraction of the tourists that come

The bay's sandy shore, particulary suitable for sun bathing on the beach and for sea bathing

The "Orbis" Monopol Hotel in Gdańsk

Groups of tourists admiring the reconstructed monuments are a daily sight in Gdańsk, especially in the Long Market

The workers of the communication system have built their rest centre in the woods near the beach at Stogi

Rest centre of the Polish National Bank at Jelitkowo

to the city. Then, where do the rest spend the night? Many of them make use of rest centres belonging to various institutions. During the summer months there are students' hotels organized in some of the students' dormitories; these are meant for students both from Poland and abroad. For school excursions canteens are set up in boarding schools or even in the school buildings themselves. Other tourists spend the night in private rooms. The number of such places varies, but the average figure is estimated at about 3,800. But all these are only half-measures. Developing hotels sufficient to meet the needs of the city and the size of the tourist movement has become an urgent necessity.

GDAŃSK RESIDENTS

In Gdańsk, 26 years after the war, there were almost 380.000 permanent residents. How did it happen that a city that was almost completely deserted as a result of the Second World War not only regained its former size but also exceeded it by over 50 per cent in that time.

Of course, the economic functions that Gdańsk obtained in the new political situation formed the basis for its development. These were related to the port, industry, administration, science, culture and service to the tourist movement. We have already discussed these functions and are now interested in the people who moved to the city in order to work in these fields.

Where did the present inhabitants of Gdańsk come from and what are they like? At first, they came from exile, from prisons and concentration camps, from the destroyed Polish cities and the nearby Kashubian villages; they were repatriated from the USSR and also from other countries to which they had been driven either by the fortunes of war or by the pre-war emigration in search of bread and work. What made these tired people, exhausted by the war and the terrible conditions of the Nazi occupation, come here, to a city in ruins, where no one could even dream of a comfortable life and where many things had to be started from the beginning?

Today, it is difficult to answer this question. There were people who came here with a definite task, to rebuild or organize life in various aspects. Some of them looked for work, others for a roof over their heads since, in a Poland destroyed by the war and the occupant, none of these problems was easy to solve. And still others simply got off the train in which they were repatriated and stayed on. There were also soldiers who had fought for Gdańsk and wished to settle here after the war had ended and demobilization was complete. Also, the **Poles** who had lived in Gdańsk before the war came here, although their number was reduced by the extermination policy pursued by the German authorities. During the progress in reconstruction and the economic development of the city, Gdańsk needed more and more workers and became the destination of those who came from other regions of Poland where there were more than enough people.

Probably only a few of the people who then came

A great many marriage ceremonies in Gdańsk are held in the Old Town Hall. Its beautiful interiors provide a magnificent setting for these solemn occasions

not come here like exiles or guests but like owners. And like owners they rolled up their sleeves and built the city from the ruins and set up its new districts. Mutual toil and mutual success, mutual worry and joy brought these people together and tied their affections to the city where they lived and worked, and which grew and became more and more beautiful before their very eyes. It was no doubt for this reason that the accidental group of people, differing not only in place of birth and accent but also often in their preferences and way of living, became a more and more unified municipal community.

During the first 20 years after the war, over 100,000 residents of Gdańsk established families here and 55,000 marriages were performed. To these, and older marriages, over 130,000 children were born in Gdańsk. This is not surprising because mostly young people came to Gdańsk and the birth rate is much higher here than in other Polish cities — in 1950 it

to Gdańsk realized that by bringing the city back to life and to Poland, they were only balancing the great account of history. To them, the Polish nature of Gdańsk was proved, not by Poland's historical rights, though they were undisputed, not by the ruins of the Gdańsk monuments ornamented with Polish eagles and the images of kings, but their own work and efforts to bring the city back to life and then develop it. However, they knew that Gdańsk had once before belonged to Poland and they did

The children of Gdańsk, although born there, no longer know what a ruined city looks like

reached as many as 30.8 per thousand (the country's average was 19.1).

As a result, Gdańsk can be called a city of young people because its residents up to 15 years of age make up 28 per cent of all the inhabitants. About 63 per cent of the inhabitants of Gdańsk are between 16 and 59 years old, (the older youth and grown-ups) and there are barely 8.8 per cent of old

Among the working people, the largest group are dockyard workers. This is what the bridge in the Gdańsk Shipyard looks like at the time when one shift finishes work

37 per cent) are people working in industry. About 22.000 are employed in building and 21.000 in transport and communication. Goods turnover gives employment to almost 17.000 people, education science and culture over 15,000 and the community

One of the several-thousand strong army of builders that restored Gdańsk to its finest shape — a master stone-cutter hewing out an element of the terrace

To provide employment for women, several industrial plants have been built. One of them is the Gdańsk Radio Works

people over 60 years old. Of course, these percentages will change as time passes.

In 1969, the number of people employed within the city was about 180 thousand. Of course, most of them are inhabitants of Gdańsk, although almost 30,000 workers come here from other cities and communities and approximately 10 thousand Gdańsk residents go to neighbouring towns, mainly to Gdynia. The largest group, over 66.5 thousand (about

The arcade constructed in Pończoszników Street (at the corner of the Long Market) to improve traffic conditions, has been adorned with keystone masks commemorating some of the architects and artists engaged in the re-construction of the Main Town

Among the arcade keystones, distinguishing itself by its place of honour and by its form, is this one representing the then Conservator of Monuments, Bronisław Mieszkow-ski; a crown is held over his head by Gdańsk's heraldic lions

and housing economy for 10,000 people. Altogether, the 5 sections of the economy mentioned supply work for 88 per cent of all people employed in the socialized economy.

Since the city is developing extremely quickly and there is a constant lack of workers, much has been done to draw women into professional activity and as substitutes for men in various posts, not only those traditionally considered feminine. Therefore, although the fact that the city is a port means employment in transport and transloading and in the shipyard industry, it does not create favourable conditions for employing women; there are as many as over 67,000 women working in Gdańsk, or over 38.6 per cent of all those employed.

The results of work depend to a large extent on the professional preparation of the workers. In Gdańsk, according to data from 1964, over 12,000 people employed in socialized plants have finished secondary trade schools and almost 11,000 institutions of higher learning. Workers with a higher technical education make up almost half of the latter group. There are many less — about 1,600 — doctors, dentists and pharmacists; the number of

Another keystone bears the effigy of the artist Professor Józefa Wnuk

economists does not exceed 1,000 nor do the numbers of specialists in other technical sciences and the humanities. From among the workers that have a higher educatioin, the largest number are employed in various branches of education, science and culture, over 2,000 are employed in industry and about 1,800 in building.

This much we can find out about the inhabitants of Gdańsk from statistics. This type of data gives a true picture, but without colour and life. To make it complete, one should present individual people, their problems and achievements. Although there are many interesting people in Gdańsk and a number of distinguished achievements, the size of this work does not permit me to discuss them, and I must leave it to other authors. This lack might be compensated at least in part by a sketchy "collective portrait" of the inhabitants of Gdańsk during the years since the war.

Historians of architecture and art, town planners and architects, constructors and plastic artists created a spatial vision of the city. What they envisaged in the place of ruins and heaps of rubble that still covered the city was brought to life by the engineers, building workers and craftsmen-artists. To fulfill these tasks the people required not only their various abilities but also complete dedication to the work. Such dedication was shown by the people who reconstructed the ceilings of St Mary's Church from platforms that hung at the level of the eighth floor to save them from falling, those who put new columns under the wavering remnants of the ceilings of Artus Court, those who mounted a slim spire on the tower of the Town Hall or placed a statue of Sigismund Augustus on its top. And what about the reconstruction of the Arsenal, the gates and other monuments? Or the building of hundred of intricately ornamented burghers' houses from their foundations? All this was done by bricklayers and concrete mixers, carpenters and various kinds of building specialists and artists — stone-cutters, smiths and plastic artists who work with metal, wood-carvers and others. Plastic artists cooperated

A cadre of Polish shipbuilders has been formed in Gdańsk. One of the laboratories at the Main Constructional-Research Centre of the Shipbuilding Industry

with them both in workshops and on scaffoldings: painters, sculptors and ceramists, both those who created new compositions and those who saved the old works of art from decay and made them complete. To a large extent these were inhabitants of Gdańsk.

The development of the city was also mainly the work of people who lived in Gdańsk — it meant new houses and factories, new communication routes and municipal equipment. Besides their normal professional activities, the inhabitants of Gdańsk devoted many thousands of hours of unpaid effort to the rebuilding and developing of their city. First, they were directed to clear the city of rubble, then to clean the streets and squares, to seed lawns, equip

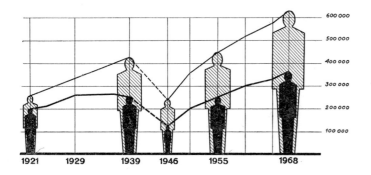

Number of inhabitants of Gdańsk and its urban complex in 1921—1968

gardens for children, to work on Westerplatte and even to do some of the building work.

The achievements of the inhabitants connected with the city are not restricted to rebuilding and developing. The achievements of the Gdańsk historians and archaeologists are also important; they throw a new light on the city's past. The work of the popularizers of history spreads knowledge about the city among the inhabitants of Gdańsk and the guests who visit it.

It would be difficult even to mention all that the inhabitants of Gdańsk have given Poland during the years since the war. It would also be difficult to find a section of the economy, science or work that lacks the participation of our city's residents. However, there are two groups whose contribution is especially great: one group consists of those who created the Polish ship industry — scientists, the people who trained the technical staff, constructors and master workers, even qualified workers. They are mostly people who gained their knowledge and experience in Gdańsk. The second group consists of scientists and engineers in the Polish turbine industry.

A ROOF OVER ONE'S HEAD

The relation of the number and quality of flats to the number of inhabitants is an indicator of the home conditions in a city and to a large degree determines the general living conditions of its inhabitants. The destruction of Gdańsk in 1945 meant that the number of flats was greatly reduced and thus the problem of a roof over one's head became a major issue.

The lack of exact data as to the flats available in Gdańsk in 1945, before the destruction, and also from the first years after the war make it difficult to determine the exact effect of the city's destruction. The way figures are quoted by various authors, the different ways of counting space — either rooms alone or with kitchens, introduces additional confusion. The figures given here were obtained by analysing the data from various sources and quoted by various authors and also by comparing them from various points of view. It turned out that it was necessary to conduct additional calculations and estimations. While the results thus gained cannot satisfy an exact tabulator or statistician, they do permit an adequate evaluation of the situation since they are free of internal discrepancies.

In 1939 Gdańsk had 66.2 thousand flats containing 148,870 rooms; 215,000 including kitchens. From the estimated amount of building during the war, the condition of the city before it was destroyed, the number of rooms can be calculated to be about 220,000, not counting barracks. Over 90,000 rooms were destroyed and many were damaged. It is difficult to evaluate how many rooms were suitable for use after the end of war activity. According to Kryński * 83,000 rooms were suitable for use in Gdańsk in 1945. This was about 54 per cent of the number before the city was destroyed. Counting kitchens, the flats available in Gdańsk after the war can, therefore, be estimated at about 120,000 rooms; this number does not include damaged roooms that were repaired by the inhabitants themselves and thus are not included in any statistics.

During the first moments after liberation these flats were sufficient because, as a result of the war

---

* Henryk Edel Kryński *Województwo Gdańskie. Studium społeczno-gospodarcze* (Gdańsk Voivodship. A socio-economic Study), *Wydawnictwo Morskie*, Gdynia, 1961.

The first — and very modest — post-war housing development in Gdańsk: a group of Finnish prefabricated frame
houses between Marx and Gdańska Streets in Wrzeszcz

and the fact that the German inhabitants had left,
the number of people living in the city dropped
from about 250,000 to 118,000. The economic tasks
of the city and the quick increase in the number
of its inhabitants caused the housing situation to
worsen and made fulfilling the mounting needs become a problem of primary importance. In the years
1945—1950 about 9,500 rooms were rebuilt and
about 6,300 were built anew, which together makes
about 15,770 rooms. During the next five years
about 2,550 rooms were rebuilt and about 14,800
were built — together about 17,350. The years
1956—1960 brought about 2,900 rebuilt rooms and
about 21,400 new ones, that is altogether about
24,300 rooms. Despite the great and constantly
growing dimensions of building, the still faster
growth of population meant that the housing situation did not improve; on the contrary, the flats became more crowded and reached 1.58 to a room or,
according to Edel Kryński*, even up to 2.38 to
a room. Not until the years 1961—1965 did the

situation improve. At that time 39,140 rooms were
built; the number of inhabitants increased by about
32,000, which meant that the flats were not quite
so crowded. In the years 1966—1969, 37,500 rooms
were built.

The following information, which includes 1945—
1969, gives a still more complete picture of the flat
building in Gdańsk at that time. During this period,
about 15,000 rooms were rebuilt and about 119,000
new ones were constructed. This means that altogether towards the end of the year 1969, 53 per cent
of all flats had been built or rebuilt after the war
and new flats accounted for as much as over 46
per cent. The average increment of rooms in the individual periods that have been mentioned above
also says a lot. They were: 2,500; 3,450; 4,850; 7,800
and 9,300. The average annual increment during
25 years after the war was over 5,400 rooms, while
the average increment in 1934—1939 was 800 rooms
a year.

Almost all flats built in Gdańsk after the war
were made by the society as a whole. In the years
1945—1948 these works were conducted by the
Gdańsk Rebuilding Management which was founded
as early as on May 1st, 1945. The Workers' Development Agency (DBOR) began its activity in 1949.
Besides DBOR, some other places of work began
to set up housing for their workers, especially after
1956. From 1957 on, flat cooperatives began to develop more and more quickly. Besides the oldest, the
Gdańsk Residential Cooperative, the following were
set up: The Teachers' Residential Cooperative, the
"Young People's Development", "Railwaymen", numerous associations building small one-family
houses and a few smaller cooperatives. Later, in
February, 1959, the largest Gdańsk cooperative and
one of the largest in Poland was set up; it was
called Przymorze (Seaside). It is worth mentioning
that this cooperative, which has excellent localities
at its disposal, has old, historic traditions. In docu-

---

* Ibid.

ments from the 13th century a settlement of the same name is already mentioned; it lay between Jelitkowo and Oliwa, beside the Oliwski Stream. In 1957, when establishing building principles, the Voivodship Town Planning Workshop used this name for the whole section that lies to the east of Oliwa. Then, the new cooperative took over the name from the area that it received.

While rebuilding, the main problem to be looked into was the technical value and the degree to which the buildings were devastated. However, here too the reconstructors tried to rebuild whole complexes at once. This made the rebuilding work easier and also ensured that the inhabitants were guaranteed better living conditions. The reconstruction based on the principles mentioned mainly covered part of the building in Siedlce, the Chełm settlement and the northern part of Wrzeszcz.

In 1947 the first new settlement was built in Gdańsk. It was a complex of 85 wooden houses that were put together on the northern edge of Wrzeszcz, between Marx and Chrobrego streets.

In 1949 the rebuilding, or rather the building of the Main Town began (it has already been described in one of the previous chapters). It was clear that this seettlement required a special approach and the proper amount of time to prepare the designs and to realize them. Thus, at the same time, the building of two other settlements was undertaken, situated on completely empty areas making it possible to use model designs on a wide scale. These were the Marx and Polish Army developments that were located on the edges of Wrzeszcz; they both derived their names from the streets on which they were located. They consist of multiple-family houses, each with three or four storeys and steep, shingled roofs. They are conveniently located as regards the communication system, shops, crèches and nursery schools. In both developments primary schools were built; in the Polish Army development it was double size — for 1,200 children — to take care of the needs of people from neighbouring areas. On the whole, the functions were properly planned in these developments, although the building arrangement is rather stiff.

The Siedlce II development was set up where the now destroyed buildings on Kartuska Street had stood. It also received a new school as well as equipment for children, and shops. The residential buildings that are three and five storeys high are mostly of model design; only a few of the buildings on Kartuska Street were individually designed. One of the functional disadvantages of the development,

Good housing conditions are provided in the Main Town even though it has been reconstructed in its original historical shape

The Polish Army housing development is situated on the border of Wrzeszcz
and Oliwa, on grounds where no buildings existed before

The reconstructed Siedlce district of Gdańsk has buildings of a rather diverisfied
character. Blocks of flats on Bema Street

A part of the Grunwald Housing Development built upon the ruins of the central part of Wrzeszcz

resulting from the shape of the ground and previous investments, is the fact that it is situated along a highway, the very idea of building along the highway is a mistake.

Two other developments that were also set up during those years are quite different. The first of them is a group of one-family houses which was built in Oliwa, in the region of Beniowskiego and Zwycięzców streets by the Building Workers' Developments Management. It consists of 38 separate and semi-detached houses. It does not have its own service equipment. The second development was built on the eastern outskirts of Gdańsk, in Górki Zachodnie and was designed for the workers of the Gdańsk River Shipyard. It consists of about a dozen two-storey houses that generally have six flats each. This development received only the most basic shops and not until later was a new school built to which the children of the neighbouring areas also go.

The reconstruction of the centre of Wrzeszcz was connected with the plan of rebuilding this part of the city. In the first years after the war, new buildings were already being set up along Grunwaldzka Street, which was widened and is part of the Gdańsk-Gdynia route. However, not until 1951 did the whole large area of over 250 acres begin to be built up. This development, called the Grunwald Housing Development, covers the centre of the district. This meant a vast programme of services. Also three new schools, crèches and nursery schools were built here. The buildings are mostly five storeys high and are located along Grunwaldzka Street; as in Siedlce they stand beside the road.

The building of the northern part of the centre of town, in which a residential development and the main service centre are located, was of primary importance to Gdańsk and was begun in 1956. This area covers the historical Old Town Osiek and part of the neighbouring areas. The compositional idea was based on building according to certain characteristics of historical architecture, which is one reason

New buildings in the Old Town; dwelling houses on Korzenna and Bednarska Streets as seen from the Old Town Hall

Another section of new architecture in the Old Town — Gdańsk's first block of flats on the Radunia Canal

why there are mostly steep ceramic roofs. At the same time, this development became a laboratory for industrial building (prefabricated elements) which imposed schematism on building. The historical buildings and the individual higher ones on the northern edge of the region, three schools and office buildings and, in the future, the main service centre offer relief from monotony.

On the opposite, southern side of the Main Town is the Stare Przedmieście (Old Suburb) development which was begun in 1960. It consists of buildings that are five, seven and nine storeys high. The composition here is quiet but contrasts with the monumental architectural forms. The outline of the Main Town, which enriches the view from within the development, is an important element in the composition. Also a school, a nursery school and part of the service centre have been built here. The southern part of the centre and the construction on the Motława have not yet been completed. Changes in the former plan were caused, among others, by the building of the Radio Works.

During this same period new buildings also appeared in Dolne Miasto (Lower Town). Between Nowa Motława and Łąkowa Street, a whole new development was built, known as Lower Town I. Since the earth is rather soft there and it is necessary to insert pales, it consists almost entirely of single nine-storey buildings. A school and district clinic were built here but the number of shops is inadequate. One of the handsomest developments in Gdańsk, named after the Defenders of the Gdańsk Post Office, was built on the eastern side of the town centre in 1959—1961. It consists of 4 four-storey buildings, 6 nine-storey buildings and the basic service equipment.

One-family houses were built in Gdańsk during the whole post-war period but developed in the years 1956—1960, when many cooperative and en-

The New Motława has been framed from the east by the blocks of flats of the Lower Town I housing development

terprise association developments were built. One might mention here the developments that lie on the borderline between Wrzeszcz and Oliwa: Jantar and the development of the Technical University employees, the development at Bażyńskiego and Polanki streets in Oliwa and the large complex along Piastowska Street. Two large complexes were also set up in the northern part of Stogi and smaller ones in the other districts of the city. Thanks to this building, the city gained a large number of rooms and some attractive sections. The bad side of this building policy was the fact that there were large

areas in between on which there were almost exclusively separate houses which require large lots.

In Gdańsk, the builders tried to combine the advantages of one-family houses with a more intensified use of the area and diminished building costs. The sets of "double row" houses are a result of these attempts (built in Stogi and in the Przeróbka development) as are the "carpetlike" houses built in Stogi. Although there were some faults, these attempts are worth mentioning as an effort to find solutions differing from the usual patterns.

The central part of Stogi that was almost com-

The Defenders of the Polish Post Office housing development situated on the eastern outskirts of the centre of Gdańsk is one of the most attractive projects in that part of the city

when typical three-storey houses were built; after 1960 an extremely varied complex was built on the shore of the Vistula: the buildings had from two to ten storeys. This solution was made possible by the various conditions of the soil on which the buildings were set up. A school and trade and crafts pavilions were built in the development but the process of redesigning and improving the development is far from being completed. The problem of building around the area of Dickman Street in Oliwa is similar. The Green Triangle development, built partly on the edge of and partly within the development of small, widely spaced wooden houses, was

The blocks of flats of the Post Office Defenders development as seen from the green square on Siennicka Street

The largest colonies of one-family houses have been built in Oliwa. The Piastowska Street development

pletely destroyed during the war waited the longest to bo reconstructed. Only a few years ago the building of a new development was begun. It will not at all resemble the fishermen's huts that used to stand here or rural cottages. Thus far, 33 multi-section and seven separate five-storey buildings have been built, as well as six buildings with ten storeys. This is approximately half of the development but already the high and varied outline of the district shows that its scale has changed. At the same time, a trade centre is being set up, a new school has been built and the old one developed and modernized.

In some parts of the city, the old, accidental buildings, or parts of buildings, are being supplemented and gradually transferred into proper developments. The Przeróbka development, the region of Dickman Street in Oliwa and the Zielony Trójkąt (Green Triangle) development are such examples. The development of Przeróbka began in the 1950's

A large residential district is rising on the site of the destroyed former buildings at Stogi, partly suburban, partly outright rural. In the background — colonies of one-family houses built a few years earlier

New buildings of the Przeróbka housing development have risen on the Dead Vistula

One of the blocks of flats accentuating the central part of Stogi. On the right — the laundry servicing the local community

given a more uniform character. Here also the five-storey, multi-section houses and the separate ten-storey buildings complete the fragmentary architecture that existed in the neighbourhood. The latter was completely detached from other residential areas and lacked services. Now, a complete structural unit has been formed. Thanks to this, the complex could have a school and a service centre.

The reconstruction of the area of Komorowski Square in Wrzeszcz that has recently been completed is of a different character. A residential complex with a service centre for this part of the district was set up here. Similar "filling" constructions on free areas or in place of destroyed buildings were erected in very many other parts of the city.

Osiedle Młodych (Young People's Development) is the most beautifully located and undoubtedly one of the most interesting of Gdańsk developments. It lies between Wrzeszcz and Oliwa on the edge of the upland and was built in 1959—1965 on an extremely varied area of over eighteen acres on the edge of a forest park. The buildings are extremely varied: 19 five-storey blocks of flats, five similar buildings with seven to ten storeys and one large building with many staircases which has nine to 11 storeys and contains 255 flats. Besides this, a school, a nursery school and a trading centre were built and both the old and the previously completed new one-family houses were altered, as was the Jantar development and the development of the

Technical University employees. However, finally the proper structural unit was achieved and thanks to its location it guarantees its inhabitants excellent living conditions.

In 1959 building began on the largest development which was supposed to house 55,000 inhabitants of the Przymorze Residential Cooperative. Located in the eastern part of Oliwa, between older buildings and the meadows on the seashore, it is an almost flat area, very convenient for building on. The planned district consists of two parts: Great Przymorze that lies to the east of Chłopska Street and the former buildings of Little Przymorze. The latter, which is completely finished and has four to nine storey houses, has 8,000 inhabitants and together with the adjoining former buildings makes up two school districts. These developments have their own trade centres and community equipment and at

The Gdańsk Young People's housing development boasts the finest location — in a rolling landscape, in the middle of a forest

The merits of its location account for the fact that the Young People's development assures its inhabitants excellent conditions for rest and beautiful views, in spite of the fact that it has been rather intensively developed

171

The Przymorze is Gdańsk's largest complex of housing projects. A part of the "A" school unit in the so-called Little Przymorze

the same time are the best managed and best kept developments in Gdańsk. In Great Przymorze the residential buildings have been completed in one of the four units; the completion of the rest will still take some time. It is within this area that the two largest residential buildings were erected; they are each two hundred metres long and have 11 storeys, 466 flats and 1,259 rooms each.

A cooperative development of railway workers has been set up in the immediate nieighbourhood of Przymorze, the region of Szczecińska and Kołobrzeska streets. It supplements the older buildings and resulted in the removal of the larger set of barracks. A small but noticeable complex of five

It is in Przymorze that Gdańsk's biggest dwelling buildings are rising. One of the so-called "flexuous" houses in Piastowska Street, with 11 storeys and 466 flats

The Millennium development at Oliwa, somewhat monotonous in appearance, yet providing proper living conditions. In the foreground — a part of the colony of one-family houses in Piastowska Street; in the background — a part of a "flexuous" house

A group of 12-storey dwelling houses on Wita Stwosza Street at Oliwa

On the Outkirts of Orunia, at the foot of the height and on the less steep parts of its slopes, the Raduńska development has risen. In the background, right — the towers of the Main Tower

slim 12-storey blocks of flats belonging to the Teachers' Cooperative was also set up in this part of Oliwa but nearer the highland, at Wita Stwosza Street.

Because the residential building could not catch up with the growing needs of the inhabitants of Gdańsk, it was decided to extend the plan for the years 1961—1965 with a simultaneous limitation on the standard of the developments. This is how the somewhat monotonous developments of five-storey buildings only came to be set up in Brzeźno, on Żuławska Street, in Orunia, on Tysiąclecia Street and partly on Wejhera Street in Oliwa. They have neither balconies nor terraces. The lowering of standards was only applied to flats. These developments, like all the others, are equipped with all the necessary services.

The development of the Gdańsk Housing Co-operative at Raduńska and Piaskowa streets in Orunia is among the newest and is still being built. It was begun in 1964 and is planned for 8,000 inhabitants. The Raduńska Development, which is situated picturesquely on the cliff and neighbours upon the old, suburban and partly rural architecture of this neglected workers' district, together with the already mentioned development at Żuławska Street and the new schools, inaugurated the rebuilding of Orunia.

This is the order in which the post-war Gdańsk residential investments were made: first rebuilding the destroyed houses and districts, then building developments on areas totally destroyed, then creating large new residential districts within areas which had never been built on before and, finally, remodelling old, poorly built districts. And although the financial means assigned for residential building purposes and also some of the regulations and norms did not allow of a perfect solution, yet the overall present architecture is much better than that which Gdańsk formerly had. Especially the installations in the flats are better.

FLATS ARE NOT EVERYTHING

Residential building, which we described in the previous chapter, gives an idea of the extent of the investments connected with fulfilling the housing needs since the war. However, the investments were not limited to flats. Those used for child care, schooling, trade, medical and other services are equally important in meeting the inhabitant's needs. These investments, which are sometimes supplementary, did not always keep pace with residential building. However, much has been done in this direction.

The fact that women are highly active professionally requires a large number of crèches to which working mothers can take their youngest children. In Gdańsk, there were 17 with 1,015 places in 1968, which means that there was one for every 22,000 inhabitants. This number is not sufficient. And at the same time, the crèches are not properly distributed: in the mid-town there is one for about 31,000 inhabitants and the Wrzeszcz and Port districts, there is one for about 20 thousand inhabitants.

The nursery schools take care of those children of working parents who are between four and seven years old. Gdańsk has 69 nursery schools now, 52 of them run by the city, 14 by places of work and two are community. Thus, there is one nursery school for every 5,400 inhabitants. Altogether, this number would be sufficient, if not for the fact that some of the nursery schools are in houses that are inappropriate and too small. Twenty new nursery school buildings have been set up. (usually for 90 or 120 children). Altogether 7,000 children are taken care of in nursery schools. Although this is a large group of children, the needs are much greater.

School building was an important and difficult problem, not only because of the quick increase in the number of inhabitants, but also because there was a large percentage of children and young people.

The necessity to modernize some of the old schools that did not meet modern requirements at all was another factor that influenced the tasks facing investments in education.

How were all these problems solved? In the 1968/69 school year, there were 80 functioning pri-

FLATS ARE NOT EVERYTHING

A nursery on Straganiarska Street in the Main Town — one of twenty for which new buildings have been erected

mary schools in Gdańsk, of which two were practice schools of the Teachers' Training Course and seven were special schools. Of the total number, 42 schools were housed in new, modern buildings erected since the war. Most of the buildings have 15 to 18 class-

The Emilia Plater elementary school on Grobla IV Street in the Main Town. The reconstructed former church of the Holy Ghost Hospital has been used for the school's main auditorium and other special rooms

rooms, not counting special rooms like laboratories. Generally speaking, primary schools had 928 classrooms, not counting P.T., and other special rooms.

New schools were built in almost all parts of the city, both in the new developments and in the old districts which showed neglect in this respect. The location of school buildings depended on the number of inhabitants who came to the various districts and on the amount of equipment already there; that

The elementary school on Żabi Kruk Street in the Old Suburb has been named after Captain Tadeusz Ziółkowski, chief of pilots of the Gdańsk harbour, murdered during the war

is how many school buildings had been saved or rebuilt. The largest number, as many as nine new primary schools, were built in Wrzeszcz, seven in the centre of town, six in Oliwa and five in Siedlce, together with Chełm and Suchanin. Two schools each were built in Brzeźno and Orunia and one each in Port, Letnica, Zielony Trójkąt, Wisłoujście, Przeróbka, Stogi, Krakowiec, Górki Zachodnie and Olszynka.

Most of the new schools were built by State investments but the community also contributed bricks. One hundred and twelve and a half million zlotys were collected in Gdańsk in the "1,000 schools for the 1,000th anniversary of Poland" campaign. From this sum, seven schools were built within Gdańsk, all monuments to the 1,000th anniversary of Poland. One of the schools was built with the help of Poles living in France. It was erected in Gdańsk and is named after Maria Skłodowska-Curie.

Besides the building of new schools, six old ones were extended: in Stogi, Błonie, Brętów and elsewhere. A few additional old schools were remodelled and completely modernized.

Despite such great efforts and imposing results the situation in the Gdańsk elementary school systems was still not satisfactory; there were still too many pupils to a classroom and some of the schools had to run two shifts. This state will improve without any further investments in the developments that are not to be developed, when the age structure of the inhabitants changes, that is after the post-war demographic boom passes. On the other hand, it is necessary to build additional schools in the new, or developing settlements and districts.

There are many various types of secondary schools in Gdańsk: 9 general, 34 vocational and technical. To give you a complete picture of the Gdańsk school system we should add that there are 8 art schools, 15 elementary vocational schools, 56 various types of schools for workers and 3 teachers' colleges. In these schools, which are partly located in old buildings and partly taking advantage of the hospitality of other schools, less construction was required. But still, 12 new buildings were set up and some of them form school complexes.

The largest complexes of this kind are the Teachers' College of Physical Training, beautifully located at the edge of the highland between Oliwa and Sopot, the great complex of the State Building Schools in Wrzeszcz, the Motor Car Technical School and the Communications Technical School in the

New schools have been built even in the most distant parts of the city. Elementary school at Krakowiec

centre of town. The former Polish Post Office of the Free City, famous for its heroic defence in September, 1939, has been adapted for the use of the last-named school's hostel.

The Economic Technical School or School of

A big complex of buildings of the Higher School of Physical Training has been built between Oliwa and Sopot. First on the left — indoor swimming pool

The Telecommunications Engineering School has been built in the Old Town
The dormitories of the Telecommunications Engineering School have been lodged in the reconstructed building of the former Polish Post Office. At the entrance — a plaque dedicated to the memory of the defenders of the Post Office

Commerce refers to the Polish traditions of the Gdańsk schooling system, to be more exact — to the tradition of Polish Schools of Commerce. It is housed in its former seat, much extended. In the old building of the Polish Secondary School there now is a Mechanical-Electric Technical School, in which mainly workers for the shipbuilding industry are trained. The Shipbuilding Technical School, the former "Conradinum" and the Basic Shipbuilding School for which new buildings have been erected on Marx Street in Wrzeszcz, also train workers for the shipyards. One should also mention here the wood, mechanical, communication, food industry and water-control technical schools. The schools that prepare the additional personnel of the health service: nurses, technical assistants and other specialists form a separate group.

Although the vocational schools of Gdańsk mentioned here do not exhaust the list, they do give an idea of the variety of these schools and the opportunities the young people have to become educated.

Higher education has already been mentioned while describing the role of Gdańsk as a scientific centre. Here, we would only like to recall that in Gdańsk there are five university-level schools: the Technical University, the Medical Academy, the Advanced Pedagogical School, the Advanced State School of Plastic Arts and the Advanced Music School.

The buildings belonging to the health service are a large section of service building, very important to the inhabitants. In Gdańsk, there are eight hospitals, of which three are clinical hospitals, three voivodship and two are specialized. The number of beds is 3,431 which means that there are nine beds to every 1,000 inhabitants. However, one should take into consideration the fact that the Gdańsk hospitals serve not only the city but the voivodship too and in some cases even beyond its boundaries.

Most of the Gdańsk hospitals, like the two Clinical Hospitals of the Medical Academy, the Copernicus Voivodship Hospital and the railway hospital, are located in their former buildings that have been partly rebuilt and in most cases developed and modernized. The Hospital for Infectious Diseases, measuring 90,000 cubic metres and covering an area of 19 hectares is a completely new building. Its building cost more than 100 million zlotys.

The modern blood donor station and the Medical Emergency Service Station are other new buildings erected for the health service. The latter has at its disposal 34 ambulances and four first-aid planes.

Out-patient treatment is given by 95 surgeries, six others clinics and hospitals, eight specialized voivodship surgeries, six district and 26 municipal centres. The others are at places of work, cooperatives, etc. In face of other, more urgent tasks, the needs of out-patients have not been fully met, both as to the number of surgeries and their quarters. Most of them are located in old buildings that have been rebuilt or altered. New buildings have been set up for two specialist's surgeries, two district and 15 regional ones. Besides these, almost 400 physicians with private practices offer medical help to the people.

A modern public home has been built in the suburbs of Gdańsk, in Lipce. Besides this, two Children's Homes have been opened in renovated buildings.

The theatres, the opera and philharmonic hall have already been described while discussing Gdańsk as a cultural centre. Besides them, Gdańsk has a few halls equipped for cabaret and other, not complicated performances. One of them is in the Maritime House of Culture in Nowy Port. The building was erected in the early 1950's and measures over 25,000 cubic metres. The architecture is somewhat bombastic and is characteristic of the building of that period. Besides the performance hall with 400 seats, it also has a small cinema, gymnasium, café, reading room and club rooms.

The Sports Hall of the Gdańsk Shipyard is another building used for various events. Although it is large, it is rather inconveniently located and is not very impressive looking; thus, it is only used as a per-

formance hall when nothing better or more appropriate can be found.

About 6,000 spectators can be seated in the 18 Gdańsk cinemas. As one can tell from these numbers, most of the cinemas are small, the average number of seats being 330. The reason for this is the large number of club cinemas and small cinema rooms in various buildings adapted for the purpose. Besides the cinema in the Maritime House of Culture, there are three new ones. The largest and most modern is called "Leningrad." It has 1,200 seats and fits quite well among the reconstructed buildings of the Main Town. There is the small *Kameralne* (Intimate) Cinema in the same building that was first supposed to be for news showings only. A new cinema was also built in Orunia. In Wrzeszcz there are four. The situation in Oliwa is the worst, for this rapidly growing district that has about 80,000 inhabitants can boast only one old, small cinema. In Gdańsk, there are 62 inhabitants to every cinema seat; in Oliwa this number is as large as about 400.

As can be seen from this short characterization, it will be necessary to build new cinemas in Gdańsk, despite the undoubted competition of television.

One of the several scores of Gdańsk's vocational schools — Secondary Shipbuilding School in Marx Avenue, Wrzeszcz

The pride of Gdańsk's health service — the modern Hospital for Infectious Diseases in Wrzeszcz, opened in 1967

These new cinemas will be needed both to serve the new districts and to replace the older ones that are inadequate and do not attract spectators.

Of course, shops and various types of restaurants were also set up in the reconstructed and newly built districts of Gdańsk, although their number is

In Nowy Port, the harbour district of Gdańsk, an imposing House of Culture has been built. It is frequented by the local community, the harbour workers and seamen

still too small. From this point of view, Gdańsk lags behind not only most of the voivodship capitals but also behind many smaller towns. Within the area of the city, there are altogether about 1,110 shops of which 1,000 are socialized. Of this number, 45 per cent are in the mid-town, about 45 per cent in the district of Wrzeszcz and about 10 per cent in the port district. Over half (57 per cent) of the shops are grocery stores. There are two department stores, both of which were built after the war in Wrzeszcz. One of the paradoxes of Gdańsk is the fact that the department store that was supposed to be built a long time ago in the centre of town has not even been started yet.

As for restaurants, the situation is not only far from being ideal, but even is far from properly satisfying the current needs. In 1969 there were 142 places serving food. They are located primarily in the shopping centres. The Gdańsk restaurants, cafés and bars vary but there is a lack of both large, really high-level eating places and the quick-service bars that are so necessary, especially during the summer season. These latter are replaced only to some degree by the 19 milk bars.

The problem of trade and food serving, besides the aspect of sufficient space, is mainly a question of where to locate and how to design these centres. Up to now, the largest centre has been set up in the centre of Wrzeszcz, along Grunwaldzka Street. This is really a district centre which has played the role of a main municipal centre for many years and still today divides this role to some degree with the centre of town.

Unfortunately, the trade and service centre in Wrzeszcz, which was built during the first years after the war, was set up in the traditional way, by building shops on both sides of the main communication route. This causes many inconveniences and since the street is on a through route, it also creates increasing trouble for both traffic and pedestrians. And sufficient space has not been assigned for parking lots and this is already becoming a noticeable and annoying problem.

The *Neptun* Universal Department Store in Wrzeszcz

One of the service pavilions in the shopping centre of Stogi

Part of the Main Town and especially Długa, Długi Targ, Piwna, Szeroka streets and the route: Węglarska, Kołodziejska and Tkacka streets form another service centre, but of a specific character. This character results from the fact that both the

buildings and the type of services, including (though still to a small degree) serving tourists, were re-created in their historical forms.

Also a few service centres have been built in new developments. The trade centre of the Polish

A section of the shopping and service centre of Wrzeszcz. In the foreground — the pavillon of the "Cristal" bar and restaurant

Shopping and service centre of Colony "A" in Great Przymorze. In the background — a part of a "flexuous" house

One of the shopping pavillons in the centre of the city — the Furniture Store in Wały Jagiellońskie Street. In the foreground — provisional stalls supplementing the still inadequate network of shops

Army Development in Wrzeszcz was built in an earlier period (the 1950's) and is one of the best; unfortunately, it has not been completed. Of the new ones, one should mention two centres in Little Przymorze which contain shop pavilions, artisan services, restaurants and community houses (a club, a library, etc.) as well as the centres of the Young People's development and Stogi. The district centres of Orunia, Siedlce and Oliwa need to be given shape to and above all a main service centre must be built in the centre of town; only its outline is marked by the shops at Rajskiej and Heweliusza streets.

THE GREEN AREAS OF THE CITY

"How much greenery you have!" visitors usually claim with envy. It is true that one gets this impression both while driving through the city and looking down at Gdańsk from higher spots — with a bird's eye view. Some parts of the city seem to be literally drowned in a green cover of trees. But at the same time, when looking through the statistical data, one can easily see that Gdańsk has only seven parks which altogether cover an area of 49 hectares, this means that there are about 1.3 square metres of park area to every inhabitant. Comparing these figures with other voivodship capitals and cities with over 100,000 inhabitants, we notice with surprise that out of 28 such cities in Poland, only seven have less park area than Gdańsk and 20 have more. Are these miracles performed by statistics? Perhaps this disagreement between observation and statistics is due to the different way the word "park" is used. In order to eliminate such differences, one should also take into consideration the municipal green lots. There are 84 of them in Gdańsk and they cover an area of 103 hectares, making altogether 152 hectares of parks and green lots in Gdańsk. This means that there are as many as 4.1 square metres of greenery to every inhabitant. And even this figure places Gdańsk only in the 21st place among those cities that have been analyzed. It is surpassed not only by cities that are known for their large amount of greenery, such as Szczecin, Poznań and Toruń but also by Warsaw, Wrocław and even Łódź, as well as some of the cities of the Upper Silesian Industrial Basin.

If this is what the statistics say then where does one get the impression of a large amount of greenery? It comes from three factors: the woods, the trees and the cemeteries.

Within the boundaries of the cities there are woods that cover an area of 33 square kilometres, which is over one-fith of the whole area of the city. A third of the woods are in forest parks. The largest and most interesting forest complex lies in the north-western part of the city, on and near the edge of the upland. The Gdańsk Zoo was founded in a valley among these woods; it is known for its beautiful location and excellent conditions for the animals. The second, much smaller, wood, although

In the northern part of the city, a big forest area borders immediately on city buildings. The forest near the Young People's development in Oliwa

it does cover 600 hectares lies between Wisłoujście and Przełom Wisły. Part of this wood grows and prevents erosion on the seaside sand dunes on which such rare and protected plants as sea holly (*Eryngium maritimum*) grow. The small and usually

The Gdańsk Zoo is well known for its fine location and the excellent conditions provided for the animals

younger forests accompany the seashore in the region of Jelitkowo and Brzeźno and the edges of the upland in the south-western part of Wrzeszcz.

The impression of rich green is undoubtedly heightened by the large number of trees that grow alone or in groups. They accompany the rivers and streams that flow through the city; they grow on the steep cliffs and along the streets; they also exist in the small gardens adjoining the houses. Probably nobody knows how many trees there are in the city altogether. We only know that in 1964 there were over 46,000 trees along the streets.

These trees are of various types and ages, among them some are rare and even very rare: the Swedish rowans, Turkish hazel-nut trees, plane

The almost 200-years old Wyzwolenia Avenue, over two kilometres long, with its four rows of linden trees, is one of Gdańsk's most precious natural treasures

trees, sword-like firs, magnolias, maidenhair and yew trees. The great linden avenue between the centre of town and Wrzeszcz — Zwycięstwa Avenue — is one of the most valuable collections of trees. It was planted almost 200 years ago. Besides its natural

Another section of Oliwa Park — one of the scenic ponds

One of the main elements of Oliwa Park — an avenue with a sea view

value, it also is of historical importance, for this is one of the last great results of town-planning from the times when Gdańsk still belonged to Poland, before it was partitioned and before Prussian rule.

The park in Oliwa is another such green monument. It was set up over two hundred years ago by the last Polish Cistercian abbot — Jacek Rybiński. This park, covering an area of 10 hectares, is named after the poet Adam Mickiewicz and is connected with a small botanical garden, though it also has interesting specimens of plants, especially trees. Most of the gardens come from that same period; the Oruński Park, Uphagen Park and the parks by the manors in Polanki, which are rather small parks than gardens and were set up near the former residences outside of town.

We have already mentioned that the cemeteries form one of the elements that create the impression of much green in Gdańsk. There are 30 of them within the city and altogether they cover an area

of 106 hectares. However, only six of these cemeteries are still being used. The Central Cemetery in Srebrzysk, on the western edge of Wrzeszcz, is the largest and most beautiful. The remaining 21 are not being used; these are mostly small ones scattered among buildings and are to be removed; there are also three war-time cemetries: the one in Zaspa, the Soviet Cemetery and the French Cemetery. The graves of the Poles murdered during the war are in the first, Soviet soldiers who died fighting for the liberatioin of the seacoast lie in the second, and the graves of French prisoners and citizens who died or were killed during the Second World War in Gdańsk or its surroundings are in the third.

The garden plots serve recreational, as well as their more practical purpose. In 1968 there were 440 hectares of them, including 29 municipal gardens covering an area of about 330 hectares. Thus, there are 12 square metres of garden plots to every inhabitant, which is much. However, this state will change, both because the number of inhabitants is increasing, and because it is necessary to build on areas now covered by gardens that stand in the way of the city's further development. Although the Gdańsk garden plots are of a strictly serviceable character and are not very spectacular from the compositional point of view, their social meaning is very important. The location of the gardens within the city depends only to a certain degree on where the inhabitants live and, to a much higher degree, on the quality and location of the areas that could be assigned for this purpose. Thus, most of such areas, over 80 hectares of gardens, are in the port district on dried-up swamps, between Wrzeszcz and Nowy Port. Oliwa holds the next place; however, many of its gardens are only temporary and must gradually give way to new buildings. There are large areas of garden plots in Stogi, Błonie, Orunia and Siedlce.

The sport areas and equipment and the beaches also serve the inhabitants of Gdańsk for recreation. The length of the seaside that can be used for sunbathing and swimming is about ten kilometres in Gdańsk, of which 1.4 is a fully equipped beach. The needs of the permanent residents and those who come here during the holiday season are much greater and this is why the whole seashore within the city is used for recreational purposes, especially during sunny holidays.

At present, the city has eight sports stadia, not counting the smaller sports grounds. The largest stadium of the Lechia Club in Wrzeszcz is an old construction that has been thoroughly rebuilt and enlarged. Also, a large stadium of the "GKKS Wybrzeże" sports club has been built almost from scrap in the Lower Town. Besides these, two other stadia have been built and a third is now under construction.

The Soviet Cemetery situated near Oliwska Gate has been designed as a part of the landscape, on the forested slopes of the elevation

The French Cemetery has been placed at the end of Legnicka Street, where a broad panorama of the historical part of Gdańsk opens up

Allotment gardens in Oliwa, between Grunwaldzka and Wita Stwosza Streets. In the background — the forested slope of the elevation

One of Gdańsk's stadiums — the old but thoroughly rebuilt stadium of the "Lechia" athletic club in Wrzeszcz

There are five sports halls in the city — three new ones and two that have been altered. With the exception of the Sports Hall of the Gdańsk Shipyard these halls are not large. Only the covered skating rink that is now being built in Oliwa will be a large hall for sports performance.

Water sports play a special role in a city that lies by the sea and also has inland waters. Sailing, rowing, boating, canoeing — all these sports make use of 11 harbours, of which five are also used by ocean liners. However, the inhabitants envy nearby Gdynia that has a large and comfortable swimming pool.

From the architectonic point of view most of the sports constructions in Gdańsk are rather modest. The more valuable examples are: the Sports Centre of the Gdańsk Technical University, which will only be completed when it has a covered swimming pool

In the fosses of the former Wisłoujście fortress, sailing boat docks are now lodged

and equipment already planned; the complex of sports halls of the Physical Training Teachers' College; and the covered skating rink.

As one can see from this brief picture, Gdańsk is not a city richly equipped with green areas. It leaves something to be desired, both as to the quantity of some types of greenery in the city as a whole, and also as to the location of the present green areas. The insufficient area of recreational parks and the complete lack of a youth park are examples of the first type of deficiency. The lack of municipal green areas in Nowy Port, the north-eastern part of Wrzeszcz and in the Lower Town are an example of the latter type of deficiency, all the more so since the distance between these parts of the city and the complex of woods makes it impossible to use them for everyday recreation.

However, with the exception of some districts, the lacks in municipal greenery are compensated for the richness of other kinds of greenery, especially by the large number of trees, including many old ones. Undoubtedly, Gdańsk has interesting and varied landscapes, as well as many areas that are not suitable for building. It is rich in trees and natural greenery; it has all the conditions which, with proper use, can create sufficient greenery to satisfy the needs of the inhabitants and bring out the beauty of the city.

THE MUNICIPAL AND PORT COMPLEX

Up to now we have been discussing Gdańsk almost exclusively. But now there is a long, almost un-interrupted belt of settlements stretching over 45 kilometres between Pruszcz Gdański and Rumia. While travelling along this belt by train or by car (the road runs parallel to the tracks), only those passengers who are aware of the local conditions know that they are passing five adjoining cities. However, even they are not always able to point out where one city ends and the next begins.

These cities: Pruszcz, Gdańsk, Sopot, Gdynia and Rumia form one municipal organism, although they do not have a common administration. These cities are called the "Gdańsk-Gdynia Complex" by the town-planners, or the "Gd" complex for short.

The Gdańsk-Gdynia complex is far from having such dimensions for it has about 650,000 inhabitants, which is less than many single cities. This comparatively small structure of settlements has a complicated spatial structure consisting of many stages and therefore it is a small, a miniature urban combine. This fact has an influence on the way the complex has been formed, which differs from the conditions of formation of most Polish cities and reminds one only to a certain degree of the cities of the Upper Silesian Industrial Basin.

In order to properly evaluate the quick development of the Gdańsk-Gdynia complex, the numbers of inhabitants that live within the present boundaries of the complex in the various years should be compared:

Year	1921	1939	1946	1950	1955	1960	1965	1970
Inhabitants in thousands (ca)	253	420	233	349	439	513	567	648

During eighteen years between the world wars (1921—1939) the number of inhabitants increased by about 167,000 of which 120,000 were from Gdynia. The war reduced the number of inhabitants to about 55 per cent of the number in 1939 and even below the number in 1921. The number of inhabitants increased due to the post-war reconstruction and development sufficiently rapidly to reach the figure for 1939 after only nine years. The present number

A section of the harbour of Gdynia. Mooring here, at the foot of the grain elevator, are the biggest ships that can enter the Baltic

of inhabitants of the "Gd" complex is 155 per cent of the number in 1939 and about 280 per cent of that in 1946.

In absolute numbers this means that in 24 years (1946—1970) the number of inhabitants of the Gdańsk-Gdynia complex increased by 415,000, almost completely without any change in the administrative borders. The extent of this increase best illustrates the

The drydock in the Paris Commune Shipyard in Gdynia which allows building of ships up to 65 thousand DWT

extent of the processes taking place here and the problems resulting from them. It also determines the role of the Gdańsk urban combine in the Polish economic body.

Gdańsk is the largest city in the agglomeration since, as we have said, it has over 380,000 permanent residents.

Gdynia is the second largest part of the complex.

Sailing dock in the harbour of Gdynia. In the background: left — one of the buildings of the Maritime School (formerly Sea Fishing School); right — the Sea Fishing Institute

Its modern artificial port was partly built on the wide peaty valley formed by the small river Chylonka and partly extended beyond the coastal line into the sea. It was rebuilt after having been destroyed during the war and was modernized at the same time. Transshipment in the port has already reached 9 million tons a year, including the largest amount of general cargo of all Polish ports, over three million tons a year. At the same time, Gdynia is the largest Polish ocean and sea-fishing base; the most modern fleet of trawler-factories is stationed here and about 30 per cent of all unloading of the fish caught in distant waters is done here. Gdynia is also a base port for our transatlantic passenger line to Canada.

Industry was comparatively badly developed during the inter-war period. At present, some basic changes have taken place in this respect. The three shipyards are the pillar of industry. The largest is the Paris Commune Shipyard which has a dry dock constructed in 1961—1962 that makes it possible to

Big repair shops of the TOS (Automobile Technical Service) in Gdynia-Chylonia

build ships up to 100,000 DTW. It also has a modern and extremely convenient technical base. The great gate crane of 500-ton capacity makes it easier to assemble ships in the dry dock. Altogether, manufacturing of means of transportation employs almost 40 per cent of the total employed in industry. The food industry plays an important role in Gdynia's economy, mainly fish and fats (over one-fourth workers are employed in this industry) as do the machine and metal construction industry and the electrical engineering industry. These four branches of industry altogether account for about three-fourth of all those employed in industry, for the total in Gdynia is 36,100 (1969).

The agencies located in Gdynia are mainly related to the maritime economy. For example, the seat of the Gdańsk Maritime Office and of the United Ocean Ports are located here. The ocean economy

The complex of sports and recreation facilities at Polanka Redłowska includes a large swimming pool

The promenade pier in Sopot is more than half a kilometre long
Grand Hotel in Sopot situated close to the beach

is also the dominating factor in other functions of the city. The Maritime School that trains officers of the merchant marine and fishing fleet testifies to this as do the Advanced School of the Navy and also the Ocean Fishing Institute, the Navy Museum and the Oceanographic Museum that is now being set up. The shipping enterprises are also connected with the fact that the city is a port — the ship-brokers, charterers and shipchandlers: the Polish Ocean Lines, Polish Ship Savers, Polcargo, Baltona, etc. The Cotton Arbitral Chamber, which deals with international matters, is mainly concerned with overseas trade.

The number of inhabitants in Gdynia reached 127,000 in 1939, fell to 74,000 after the war, exceeded the pre-war state in 1955 and is now higher by over one-third. Thus, the increase in the number of inhabitants during the post-war period is 100,000.

New developments have been built for the new inhabitants. They were set up as a supplement to the architecture of the centre of town, on Nowotki Hill, in Witomin, Grabówek, Chylonia and Oksywie. Altogether, about 76,500 rooms were built in Gdynia in the years 1945—1967. During the inter-war period, Gdynia was a surprising combination of contrasts caused by the fact that from a village it was becoming a city. These contrasts can still be found today, though the new architecture is gradually erasing them and is making more and more sections of the city look uniform and finished.

The new architecture and the development of the number of inhabitants required investments in communications, the sewage system, water conduits and power. Thus, part of the mid-town communications system was improved, new water intakes and sections of water conduits and new power lines installed. Since it was impossible to extend the former sewage system which had been too carefully planned, a new sewage-treatment plant, a large main drain and a few pumping stations were built.

In Gdynia, as in Gdańsk, the forests that adjoin the city from the west form the greatest concentration of greenery. The part on the slopes of Kamienna Góra set up a few years ago is a beautiful section of Gdynia — from the top of the hill there is an excellent panorama of the city and port. There will also be interesting views from the seaside avenue that is now being built at the foot Kamienna Góra.

Sopot, which lies between Gdynia and Gdańsk, was once a seaside resort and is now becoming more and more a residential district of the "Gd" complex. It also has the additional functions of a tourist centre. The tourists are served here by the large seaside Grand Hotel and a few smaller hotels and boarding houses, as well as a tourist centre of the Polish Tourist Association, a few rest centres owned by various institutions and camping sites.

Besides the picturesque location between the edge of the wooded highland and the sea, Sopot has the following tourist attractions: a promenade pier which is over half a kilometre long, a beautiful sandy beach and the beautiful Forest Opera which existed here before but has been completely remodelled, equipped and covered with a roof made of a special fabric. The theatrical performances, concerts and other events that take place here, including the International Song Festival, have a special charm that is the main characteristic of this place.

The administrative and service pavilion of the tourist centre in Kamienny Potok, run by the Polish Tourist Association and serving mass excursion traffic

The beautiful located Forest Opera in Sopot has been modernized and covered with a plastic roof

The Heroes of Monte Cassino Street in Sopot, reconstructed and reserved for pedestrian traffic only

The "Alga" restaurant pavillon

Building of the County People's Council in Pruszcz Gdański. In the background — construction of a new housing project

Sopot, which had about 31,000 inhabitants before the war, has grown comparatively little and now has about 48,000 inhabitants. However, its tourists considerably raise this number during the summer months. From the point of view of employment, Sopot is not self-sufficient and most of its inhabitants work in the neighbouring cities, especially in Gdańsk.

The post-war residential architecture that not so long ago consisted almost exclusively of one-family houses, is concentrated on the southern and western sides of the city and in Kamienny Potok. At present, larger complexes of multiple-family houses are being built within the region of Malczewskiego and 23 Marca streets. Also some public buildings have been constructed in Sopot, including four elementary schools and a new buliding and a large students' hostel of the Advanced School of Economics.

Rumia is the part of the complex lying furthest to the nord-west. During the inter-war period, there were a few villages here but they began to become urban suburbs under the influence of neighbouring Gdynia which was then developing. In 1954 Rumia, which then had about 11,000 inhabitants, received municipal rights. The fact that its urban character was recognized too late and the private speculations on land, both had a great influence on the character of the architecture and the way the city was planned. Although it now has more than 23,000 inhabitants, most of the buildings are one-family houses covering a large area. Only in the 1960's were settlements of multiple-family houses built on the empty areas in the centre of the city. Planned and intelligent building was made difficult by the lack of a municipal sewage system, which Rumia is just now receiving and which is being connected with the new Gdańsk purifying plant. The existing water conduits, still insufficient, are also connected with Gdynia.

There are three industrial plants in Rumia: the Shipping Equipment Factory, the Tannery and the cooperative boiler factory. Nevertheless, not many people can be employed and most residents commute to work in Gdynia. In 1945—1967 residential building produced about 9,000 rooms in Rumia, which is over 60 per cent of the present number.

On the opposite, southern side of the "Gd" complex lies Pruszcz. This is the smallest city of the urban "combine." In the Middle Ages, Pruszcz was already a large village on the road to Gdańsk. Its meaning to Gdańsk was based on the fact that a canal branched off from the Radunia River here and brought water to the Gdańsk mills and other workshops operating with water. Although Pruszcz was very conveniently located, it remained a village up to the Second World War, partly because it had been destroyed during most wars. Neither the building of roads and railway tracks, nor the large sugar refinery erected in 1880, changed its rural character.

In 1941, Pruszcz was included in the administrative boundries of Gdańsk. However, this did not have any influence on its development and building within it. After the war Pruszcz, which was destroyed and had less than 3,000 inhabitants, was acknowledged as an independent town and in 1950 it became the seat of the district administration. This fact, as well as the setting up of several industrial plants, warehouses and bases, mainly connected with serving agriculture, made the city develop and it now has reached 12,500 inhabitants. During the post-war years two groups of one-family houses have been built in Pruszcz, as well as two multiple-family settlements, altogether containing 3,400 rooms. Besides this, a number of public buildings to meet the needs of the administration and the school system have been erected. The development of the city has been limited by the lack of sewage and municipal water conduits. Only in 1966 was the building of this equipment begun.

The Gdańsk urban combine is not at all uniform, as even this short description demonstrates. However, it does have many and various connecting links. As a result, there is a close interdependence in the development of various parts of the urban combine, not only as concerns the inhabitants but also the municipal engineering and communication equipment. Thus, what has been happening for some twenty-five years now in spatial planning — treating the complex as a whole — sooner or later must be reflected in the administration. Some steps in this direction have already been taken.

INCREASING TRAFFIC MEANS INCREASING PROBLEMS

The network of streets in Gdańsk which has been growing for ages and was not properly planned while the suburbs were expanding, already showed serious shortcomings during the inter-war period. Also in Gdynia, the communication system could have been better, even though this is a city that has been built from scrap in the 20th century. These deficiencies resulted from the fact that the number of inhabitants was expected to be lower than it is and by the financial difficulties of the municipal economy.

With such a "hereditary handicap," which was increased by the devastations of the war, Gdańsk and Gdynia entered a new stage of development in 1945. This stage of a growing urban combine created completely new problems and a new scale of communication needs. For the requirements of a city with 250,000 inhabitants, such as Gdańsk was before the Second World War, were different from the needs of a municipal complex with 380,000 inhabitants.

Problems connected with collective communication began to accumulate first. Almost from the first days after liberation, the new political and economic situation and the fact that the devastated areas were unevenly located made it necessary to transport passengers along the route connecting the cities of the complex and especially along the part connecting Gdynia and Gdańsk.

To fulfill these needs the decision to build was taken shortly after the war and in 1950—1954 an electric railway line connecting the cities of the "Gd" complex was built parallel to but separate from the existing railway system. In the following years, this system was lengthened from Gdynia to Wejherowo, this time on the same tracks as the long-distance train. Altogether, the length of the electrified local system is 52 kilometres and the small distances between stops (usually from one to two kilometres), as well as the frequent traffic, give it the character of a fast local municipal train.

Rebuilding, development and setting up new places of work and building new settlements and residential districts, together with the growing functional integration of the complex, mean that the passenger traffic steadily increases on the routes lead-

In spite of the fact that the electric railway is the predominating means of transport for those commuting to and from work, the trams of Gdańsk carry twice as many passengers annually as the railway

ing through it. Now, when over 70,000 people travel every day on the most crowded part of the electric railway line, and 16,000 travel during the rush hour, the previous frequency of trains — every 7 to 8 minutes — is no longer sufficient. This is why it became necessary to modernize the local system. It was done by introducing an automatic block system

The main street of Wrzeszcz — Grunwaldzka, twice as wide now as it was before the war, makes part of the system of roads linking the cities of the Gdańsk-Gdynia urban complex

and increasing the frequency to every 6 minutes, which in the future will even become 3 minutes.

The dominant role of the electric train in taking people to work results from its location in the body of the municipal complex. The train reaches an area in which are 40 per cent Gdańsk's places of residence and almost 50 per cent of the whole "Gd" complex. There is a still larger percentage of places of work: 48 in Gdańsk and 56 in the urban combine.

The most important problems connected with commuting were solved by the building of the local electric railway. However, this does not mean that all the communication needs were satisfied, even in the field of collective communication alone. This seeming paradox can be explained by the following comparison: altogether in 1968 (not counting long-distance trains), 281 million passengers were carried within the Gdańsk-Gdynia complex and of this number the electric train and the local steam train carried a little over 20 per cent. What about the rest?

Over 121 million passengers, that is, 43 per cent travelled on the Gdańsk trams. It is worth noting that this is almost four times as many as in 1938. The length of the tram lines has not changed radically and the increase in the number of passengers has been made possible by modernizing the stock and some of the routes. The latter consisted in replacing one-track by two-track lines (the East-West route in mid-town, Wrzeszcz, Brzeźno, partly Oliwa-Jelitkowo, Kartuska Street) and the tracks were separated from the roadway (Grunwaldzka Street, Podwale Grodzkie, Wały Piastowskie, Leningradzka Avenue). The trolley buses in Gdynia correspond to the Gdańsk trams and to some extent they also serve Sopot. However, only 16 per cent of all the passengers use them. On the other hand, bus communication develops quickly and continuously within the whole complex. Today, 22 per cent of the passengers travel by bus, or over sixty-one million people annually.

Street traffic and the problems connected with it — the need to rebuild old streets and to construct

In the past, all east-west traffic had to squeeze through this Golden Gate opening, only three metres wide, like through the proverbial needle's eye. It was blocking at the same time the historical layout of streets in the Main Town, ill-adapted to present needs

The traffic is mainly concentrated on the only communication route connecting the cities of the complex, as a result of the spatial structure of the urban complex and also of the fact that the street system is not properly developed. In addition, this route was not at first sufficiently wide and was technically unsatisfactory. But in 1947—1950, it was already widened, taking advantage of the space made by war devastations in the centre of Wrzeszcz. In 1948 similar changes were made on the Sopot-Orłowo section of the route. Not until the 1960's was work continued on the part joining Wrzeszcz, Sopot and Oliwa, as well as in the centre of Gdynia. In 1965 the whole route from Gdańsk to Gdynia, 18 kilometres long, had been widened. It was high time, since the peak traffic had already exceeded 1,500 vehicles an hour in one direction.

Equally important problems existed in the centre

A few years ago, the traffic was shifted to a new east-west thoroughfare, called Leningradzka Avenue, and built along the historical Podwale Przedmiejskie route and the lines of fosses of the Main Town

new ones, exist along with the matters described above and although in the beginning these problems were not so drastic, they are now becoming more and more urgent. Above all, the traffic depends on the number of vehicles. In 1939, there were less than 6,000 mechanical vehicles registered in Gdańsk. Now, there are nearly 30,000 and the number is constantly increasing. The fact that the traffic from neighbouring cities is concentrated in Gdańsk as the main city of the urban combine and the fact that many tourists come by car during the summer, also affect the amount of traffic in the city.

Podwale Grodzkie Street in front of the Main Station, completely rebuilt, with a separate tram trackway and six traffic lanes has a traffic capacity three times greater than before

of Gdańsk. The appropriate routes of the new roads were already anticipated when the reconstruction was planned. Their realization, which depends on the increasing needs and the current possibilities, will last a few years more. But even though what has already been done represents only a small per cent of the planned and necessary investment, the form and conditions of communication in the centre of town have already been considerably improved.

Among the most important communication investments in the mid-town are: building Leningradzka Avenue, the new entrance route from the south, rebuilding Podwale Grodzkie, together with building the Piastowski Junction, constructing the new Trzeciego Maja Street and building the new "Błędnik" viaduct which is now under construction and which

will be much wider, as well as the thorough remodelling of the Oliwska Gate junction. The construction of Leningradzka Avenue, a modern two-way road with separate tram tracks that forms the middle section of the planned east-west route, made it possible to divert all traffic from Długa Street and to limit it to Długi Targ. Some advantages of this new route will only become noticeable when the eastern section is built together with a second bridge and when it is extended towards the west.

The entrance to the centre of Orunia, that used to be the municipal section of the road from Silesia to Poznań, was narrow and full of turns. In 1962—1964 a new, wide viaduct and a new section of the road were built which lead traffic into the city directly and are part of the planned structure.

One of the elements of the reconstructed communication system of the centre of Gdańsk is the junction at the intersection of Rajska, Wały Piastowskie and Podwale Grodzkie Streets

To eliminate collisions of pedestrian and vehicle traffic in front of the Main Station, a wide underground passage for pedestrians has been built with direct access to tram stops

Jedności Robotniczej Street in Orunia, also a part of the main route, can serve as illustration of the tasks still waiting to be solved

The work connected with rebuilding Podwale Grodzkie was the biggest. Here, in front of the Main Station, a narrow road inconvenient for traffic with tram tracks in the middle, was replaced by a wide road with three traffic lanes and separate tram tracks. All this was done by demolishing a few remaining houses. At the same time, a modern communication junction was made to replace a bad crossing. The tram-stop islands were made much wider and in order to avoid collisions with pedestrians, a tunnel was built under the street, 9.5 metres wide, leading to the tram stops. A similar tunnel was built under Trzeciego Maja Street, opposite the station. The tunnel under the station and an escalator will connect the two tunnels, which will ease the traffic to and from the station.

To complete the picture of communication investments in the mid-town, one should also mention Wały Piastowskie — a section of the new road leading to the shipyards, and the new streets Rajska and Heweliusza — which form the basis of the communications structure of the northern part of the mid-town and the planned service centre, as well as the lengthening of Toruńska Street which improved communication in the Old Suburbs and the southern part of the Lower Town.

Apart from the centre other works have been done, such as: modernization of the eastern part of Elbląska Street, building of major Sucharskiego Street which leads to Westerplatte, reconstruction of Kartuska Street and widening of Jedności Robotniczej Street.

One of the new depots — the PKS (Long Distance Bus) station in Oliwa

The development of the network of streets in the new districts is a different problem, though it is equally important. Besides those built in the settlements in various parts of town, the most important were in Oliwa where Kołobrzeska Street, and part of Piastowska and Chłopska streets were constructed in connection with building Przymorze. The fact that the viaduct on Kołobrzeska Street, built only fifteen years ago, recently had to be widened, is a proof of the rapid development of communication needs. Also in Wrzeszcz, the construction of new settlements made it nesessary to build another lane on Marx Avenue and to surface Wojska Polskiego Street.

All the communication investments here described had a great influence on the conditions of traffic in the city and although they still did not create a new communication structure, they consistently approach it. Above all, the plan of the structure includes developing the communication routes along the complex: widening the southern (Jedności Robotniczej Street in Gdańsk) and northern (Czerwonych Kosynierów Street in Gdynia) edge of the present through-route; building new roads parallel to the main route, among them the "Green Route" along the seaside, that would shorten the way from Nowy Port to Sopot and Gdynia and, finally, building an express road with overhead crossings called the "Red Route" in the more distant future. A road by-passing the complex would serve lorries going to the northen districts of Gdańsk and to Sopot and Gdynia and thus would lighten the municipal traffic. It could also be used by the suburban settlements in the western surroundings.

The developing set of perpendicular and ring roads connecting the individual districts without going through the centre of town also play an important role in the planned structure. Some of these roads would serve to render the communication service of the port efficient, for its western and eastern parts have larger prospects for development.

The problem of parking lots is only now being worked on in practice, though much attention has been paid to it. A few parking lots have been built in the mid-town and some special squares for parking at the Zoo and the beach in Stogi — places that especially need them. For the present state of motorization, the number of parking places is on the whole sufficient but since the needs are growing rapidly, a systematic realization of the plans for parking lots is indispensible.

The number of garages and service stations has also been increased, though not sufficiently. On the whole, the garages for cars are not very big and are usually located in residential developments. Larger garages have been built for transport enterprises. There are seven such garages in Gdańsk, accommodating 100 to 300 vehicles, not counting those bases of the stock belonging to other enterprises. The needs of a technical basis for motorization will also continue to grow. The decisions made in long-term planning determines their extent. The expected number of 90 cars to every 1,000 inhabitants decided upon in the plans will, however, probably have to be increased in the future. These changes also influence all the problems of communication; the remodelling and developing of the old-fashioned, former structure, are among the most important town-planning and investment plans for Gdańsk and the whole urban combine.

BOTH ABOVE AND UNDER THE EARTH

Most municipal installations hidden under the earth which leads them to be taken for granted and the inhabitants of a city only become interested in them when they fail to work properly. In the meantime, everything that lies under the large cities is not only of elementary importance to the proper functioning of municipal bodies but also exceeds many an investment carried out on the surface of the earth in its scale and the costs of construction.

The post-war rebuilding and development of Gdańsk and the whole urban combine could not have been done without large investments in this field too, so let's take a brief look at them.

The Gdańsk water conduits, or, to be more exact, the present water system, was started a hundred years ago. Further development without a uniform plan created a complicated system which lacked uniformity and which was based on seven different types of water intakes; because of the differences in height it was divided into three pressure levels. In 1937 the Gdańsk water conduits were 281 kilometres long and 7.96 million cubic litres of water were produced. The post-war development of the city and the better flat equipment (bathrooms, hot water installations) caused a rapid increase in the demand for water. To fulfill these needs, the three old water intakes were developed and in 1960—1965 a new one, the largest in Gdańsk, was built. It could supply 35,000 cubic metres of water a day. In 1969 the production of water was 34.6 million cubic metres which is 435 per cent of 1937 production. The total per capita use of water has tripled.

The pipes of the sewage system were 217.5 kilometres long before the Second World War. After the war, destruction was repaired and extension begun. This was necessary not only because of the increase in the number of inhabitants but also because the flats were better furnished with sanitary equipment. The length of the sewage system increased to 438 kilometres and, counting the pipes in individual flats, to 392 kilometres. The purification plant was also developed and modernized. Also the constructions has begun on the main drain for the cleaning of sewers.

The power industry is a separate field in municipal installations; it covers gas engineering, electric energy and heating. Gas engineering, which is the oldest form of transmitting energy to a distance, is no longer the most important type of energy, though it still plays an important part in the household. Gdańsk had a comparatively new gas station which was built at the beginning of the 20th century in the northern part of the town centre. After the devastations of war were removed, this gas station was able to meet the city's needs for some time but as early as in the 1950's its production had to be increased. Although the development made it possible to increase the production from 26.6 million cubic metres before the war and reached 80 million cubic metres in 1969, it did not satisfy the growing needs. In this connection, it was decided to build a long pipeline to carry natural gas from southern Poland.

Electric energy is the most universal and the most rapidly developing part of the power industry. In 1937, 61.8 million kilowatt hours were used within the whole area of the Free City Gdańsk and in 1968 this number increased to 369 million kilowatt hours in Gdańsk alone. These numbers best illustrate the dynamic development. A far-reaching high voltage network was developed to meet the quickly growing demand. Before the war, the highest voltage on lines supplying a city was 60,000 volts, now it is 220,000 volts. Current is supplied at this voltage from the complex of electric power stations in the Konin Basin and is then transformed to 110,000 volts and is thus fed to the distribution centres of the Gdańsk urban combine. Gdańsk itself has five such feeding points. Also, the distribution systems of high and low voltage had to be remodelled and developed for they were working chaotically and at various voltages, sometimes they even supplied direct current. Now a uniform system of distribution systems of alternating current is being introduced: 15,000 volts in the municipal lines of high voltage and 380-220 volts for the recipients.

Before the war, most of the Gdańsk flats were heated by stoves, some of them by a separate installation of hot water heating for each floor and only a few buildings had central heating with individual furnace rooms. After the war, all the new multiple-family buildings of flats and public utilities were equipped with central heating. At the beginning, these installations were supplied from the settlement boilers, but later the power station was converted into a heat and power generating plant and a municipal heating system was built to supply most of the mid-town. In the districts further out, settlement boiler houses were still being built, but most of them were to be done away with after the new, large heat and power generating plant, already started, was finished. In 1964 the Gdańsk Heating Enterprise administered 45 kilometres of pipes and the heated buildings totaled over four million cubic metres. The development of this branch of the power industry does much to increase comfort, not only by eliminating heavy work, but also by diminishing the pollution of the air in the city. The development of central heating is also of great economic importance, for it enables a sensible use of fuel.

The description of the underground installations of a modern city would not be complete without telecommunication installations. Although the main sections are above ground, the network of underground cables increases constantly. They connect the individual exchanges with the subscribers and the city with other cities. Instead of the former overhead networks or the cable laid in the ground, a special system of cable canals is now being built. The Gdańsk telecommunication network is already an integral part of the automatic junction that covers the whole municipal complex. This junction, still being developed, is to cover all the towns in Gdańsk Voivodship and guarantee automatic connection with Warsaw and other larger Polish cities.

As part of the realization of this plan, four new municipal exchange and an international exchange have been built in Gdańsk itself. New exchanges have been set up also in Gdynia, Sopot and Pruszcz. Telecommunication is a field that requires constant development, both of the equipment built on the ground as well as of the networks that are hidden under the earth.

AN ATTEMPT AT SUMMING UP

The Second World War destroyed thousands of cities and towns. Gdańsk was one of those which were most destroyed: the overall devastation reached 60 per cent, the port was destroyed and blocked, industry was ruined, the mid-town was turned into a desert of rubble; there was no communication, water, gas, electricity. Since 1945, when the city experienced the greatest cataclysm of its history, a quarter of a century has passed. What has been done in this time?

The state of the city after the war would cause even the greatest optimist to doubt whether it would be possible to bring it back to life again. But these doubts turned out to be unjustified. Gdańsk is alive. What is more, in many fields the rhythm of life is much greater than before the catastrophe. Therefore, let's recall the most significant facts and figures.

In 1938 there were 21,300 people working in industry and in 1969 there were 66,500, or three times as many! The shipyards are a typical example of the development of Gdańsk industry. The ships the Gdańsk shipyard produced in 1965 together had a total of 197,200 DWT, while before the war the annual production of both the shipyards which formed the basis of the present one averaged a little over 20,000.

The warehouses of Gdańsk port administered by the Port Council covered 98,100 square metres in 1938 and 3,000 square metres in 1945, while the Port Administration had storehouses covering 81,000 square metres in 1965. The amount of transshipping equipment, which dropped to four items in 1945 from 99 in 1938, was increased to 120 (together with floating and self-propelled cranes). At the same time, the port was reconstructed; it was also modernized and adapted to serve large ships. Therefore, although the transshipments have not reached the former level, we can expect that the great hydraulic engineering works now being conducted in the port will cause a rapid development in the next few years.

A great, almost unbelievable advance can be observed in science. Gdańsk, with its two institutions of higher learning and 1,500 students, was a third-rate centre before the war. Now it has six institutions of higher learning, approximately 17 thousand

This is how the centre of Gdańsk, destroyed in 90 per cent during the war, now looks. In the foreground — the Old Suburb; in the background — the Main Town

students and over 2 thousand scientific workers, as well as 31 scientific research centres. Similar changes have occurred in Gdańsk's role as a cultural and tourist centre.

All this had made the city develop immensely. The number of inhabitants offers the best proof: from about 120,000 in 1945 it increased to 378,000 in 1970. This means an increase of almost 260,000 in 25 years, and of about 128,000 inhabitants as compared to 1939. Thanks to this increase in the number of inhabitants, Gdańsk had advanced from eight to sixth in size among the cities of Poland, overtaking Bydgoszcz and Katowice. It is also worth noting that this development did not take place at the cost of other cities of the voivodship. The inhabitants of Gdańsk accounted for 32.2 per cent of the municipal inhabitants of Gdańsk Voivodship in 1946 and this number had increased to approximately 36.7 per cent in 1969, even though the number of inhabitants of the remaining cities had increased by over 380,000 during the same perod. On the basis of these figures, we can easily tell that as far as the population of the city is concerned, the period of reconstruction finished in 1956 and since then the city has been developing.

However, the number of inhabitants is only one standard, so let's compare the supply of flats. In 1939 they contained only about 215,000 rooms and in 1969 — 252,500 rooms. Comparing the number of inhabitants and rooms in 1939 and 1969, we notice that there are more people to a room than before the war. This is an undesirable phenomenon which is caused by the large devastations on the one hand and the rapid development of the city on the other. The increase in building, six- and in the last years even ten-fold in comparison with before the war, has not managed to meet the growing needs but is only an additional proof that they are growing extremely rapidly.

Also in the field of service and public utility investments, a great effort has been made. Limiting ourselves to the most important positions, we should mention the 11 crèches, 20 nursery, 42 elementary,

Decisive for the reconstruction and rise of the city has been the growth of the Polish maritime economy. A part of the Lenin Shipyard in Gdańsk

The harbour of Gdańsk is throbbing with life. Ships in the Władysław IV dock

The historical monuments of the Main Town, raised from ruins, again charm with their beauty as in the times of greatest glory

The expanding city is cramped for room within its old confines. Big new districts are rising. The Przymorze development under construction (1966)

The city is growing not only in breadth but upwards as well — the scale of its buildings is changing, former suburban houses are being supplanted by new blocks and districts. A section of the Green Triangle housing development

In the centre of the city, on grounds reserved for this purpose in Rajska Street (which can partly be seen in the lower left part of the picture), a shopping centre will be built comprising a department store, a quick-service bar, numerous stores and a big hotel, the House of Technicians, and an office building

and 12 secondary schools, 1 new and 4 extended hospitals, as well as 21 other buildings belonging to the health service, a theatre, a house of culture, 3 cinemas, an indoor swimming pool, 3 sports halls and also over 30 other public buildings. Nevertheless, there is still a lack of services in Gdańsk, especially in trade. But this is not surprising, especially if we take into consideration the fact that in all cities these services are mainly concentrated in the centre of town, which in Gdańsk was 90 per cent destroyed.

Rebuilding monuments was an especially difficult problem in Gdańsk, not only because of the need for material resources. The Gdańsk group of monuments was one of the largest and most valuable and its devastation was an irreparable loss to European culture. The action of securing and rebuilding monuments that was undertaken almost immediately after the war activity ended and was continued for many years yielded results that speak for themselves. Looking at Gdańsk today it is difficult to realize what it was like in 1945. The enclosed photographs give some idea of the extent of the work done and of how the city changed in twenty-four years. However, it is impossible to document in this way all the reconstruction work that has been done because the number of buildings that were rebuilt is too large. Therefore, let's try to sum up briefly: 6 municipal gates and 1 foregate, 9 towers, 4 churches, 6 granaries and 12 larger public buildings have all been rebuilt; besides this, a few hundred historical buildings of flats have been reconstructed, mainly from the ground up. Also, the damage done to 3 defence gates, 1 tower, 2 churches and 1 granary has been repaired. The following monuments have been rebuilt in part: 4 towers, St Catherine's, St Bartholomew's, the Holy Trinity, St. John's and St. Barbara's churches, as well as the Wisłoujście Fortress; the Cow's Gate, the remnants of Świętojańska and the Holy Ghost gates, St. John's, St. Bridget's, SS. Peter and Paul's and St. Barbara's churches and finally a few granaries have only been preserved. And one must not forget that the problem of fully reconstructing certain monuments is not only a question of financial means and resources, but it also concerns the difficult work of artists and craftsmen which cannot be hastened at will.

Besides the historical complex, many new developments and the larger part of the great residential district Przymorze have been built in Gdańsk. They are new spatial elements of the city; they are impressive for their impetus and introduce new values. At the same time, there are empty spaces on areas that were formerly built up, which have remained after the buildings were destroyed. Why have they not been filled in yet? This could have been done easily if "rebuilding at all costs" was the main aim, but would it be right? In this way the opportunity to remodel the city after the devastations would be lost, the opportunity to correct former errors and to adapt the city to its new and future needs. This is why the principle was adopted of reconstructing only where there were no objections to the former set-up and of creating new buildings only on areas appropriate to their functions. This is why new areas were made use of while some of the old ones remained empty as a reserve for future development or for provisional building. This is a much more difficult and undoubtedly less spectacular method, but it is the only right one in relations to the distant future. Already the application of this principle has made it possible to remodel part of the communication structure and the segregation of individual functions and structural units has improved living conditions.

Were any mistakes made while shaping the new profile of the city? The future will give the proper answer to this question. Some mistakes could not be avoided; we have spoken about them in previous chapters. But the general principles have been accepted and well carried out. As a result, the new Gdańsk, a new municipal body which is growing before our very eyes, is to preserve everything good and beautiful that has been done in it throughout the centuries and is to remodel everything else, change it and develop it as required by the needs of the present and the future.

THE SHAPE OF TOMORROW

As day follows day, the future becomes the present and the present becomes history. And only by taking into consideration development prospects does it become possible to evaluate our activity properly. Let's try to unveil the future of Gdańsk, if only in a general outline.

Let's start from the immediate future, which is determined to a large extent by the investments already assigned. Thus, in the mid-town, most important is the final completion of the reconstruction of the Main Town and at the same time an administrative trade centre to be built at the Coal Market. Within the former Old Town, a main service centre with the Central Department Store, a hotel, quick-service bar and trade pavilions, as well as the Technician's Home and office skyscrapers belonging to enterprises connected with the maritime economy will be set up on grounds that are reserved for this purpose. The few remaining free areas will be taken by a large group of administrative and trade buildings. A large administrative complex planned and already begun in Podgórze can only be finished after the east-west route is prolonged to the west

(Leningradzka Avenue) and this, in turn, depends on the alteration of the railway tracks that run through the centre of town.

A new bus station for long-distance and local buses, conveniently connected by a tunnel with the railway station, will be built north of this complex, at Trzeciego Maja Street; later, administration buildings and possibly a tourist hotel will be set up.

The eastern part of the centre — the Lower Town — will receive a new residential development situated along the new Motława and prolonged towards the east of Leningradzka Avenue. The industrial plants that exist in this part of the city will then be improved and the belt on the side of the river and the former bastions will be made into green plots.

Granary Island is the part of the mid-town that will probably have to wait to be built up. The increase in the tonnage of ocean-going vessels deprived the Motława of its role as port waters and Granary Island of its transshipment and storing functions. Since it does not have the appropriate conditions for residential functions, and its central location makes it an especially valuable area, it has been destined for the mid-town supply-technical centre; it will also be used for administrative and hotel purposes and for an inland sailing and coastal navigation harbour. However, it is still difficult to state when the planned investments will be realized and will replace the buildings that have been located there temporarily.

There will be many changes around Zwycięstwa Avenue. First of all, the avenue itself will have to be rebuilt. Of course, adapting it to the growing communication requirements must be accomplished without destroying this wonderful natural monument. The sports complex of the Gdańsk Technical University will be finished along the avenue, and also the Opera House will be remodelled and developed. A complex of buildings belonging to the Theoretical Institute of the Medical Academy and a few new buildings of the Technical University will be set up on the neighbouring grounds. The basic development of the Technical University will include the areas to the west and south of the school (towards Suchanin).

The changes will not be large in Wrzeszcz because the condition of the buildings in this district does not permit of any large investments. However, here too new buildings will be set up in place of the old ones on Partyzantów Street and Świerczewskiego Square. There will be a service centre with a large parking lot and a pedestrian passage under Grunwaldzka Street which is very necessary here. The new service pavilions will also be built on the northern side of the pedestrian route which begins at the railway station and which has recently been thoroughly altered. Improving the communication structure is an important and difficult problem that involves the plan to build a new sequence of streets (Partyzantów, Chrzanowskiego, Polanki), to widen Słowackiego Street and to modernize the junctions of Grunwaldzka — Kościuszki and Grunwaldzka — Wojska Polskiego streets and especially to build a road for external traffic to the western part of the port, by-passing the mid-town area.

A dwelling, shop and office building at the corner of Grunwaldzka and Partyzantów Streets in Wrzeszcz. The photo shows its model.

A large group of buildings of the Teachers' College will be erected between Wrzeszcz and Oliwa; our photo shows its model. The construction of students' dormitories (background) has already been started

In the vicinity, a covered ice-rink is being built. This is what it will look like when completed

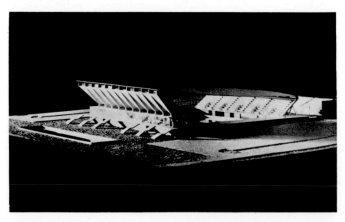

A great complex of buildings belonging to the Gdańsk University will be built between Wrzeszcz and Oliwa. It is planned that this complex will in time become a university, so needed in the northern part of Poland. In the meantime, a covered artificial skating rink and a sports stadium will be completed on the neighbouring areas.

The building of Przymorze, the great cooperative residential district that, together with the smaller developments that are being erected in the neighbourhood, will have about 75,000 inhabitants, will be finished during the next few years in the eastern part of Oliwa. As to other districts, the developments in Brzeźno, Stogi and Orunia will also be finished and the development called "Siedlce III" will probably be built on the western side of Kartuska Street. A new part of the port to serve the largest vessels coming to the Baltic will be constructed.

Industry will mainly develop in the port areas and those next to the port, partly also in Orunia. A certain number of less intrusive plants that serve the city will be set up on special areas near the residential districts.

A few scientific-research centres like the Hydroconstruction Institute, the Flow-Machines Institute and the Maritime Electric Engineering Plant will receive new buildings to meet their needs. A large Centre of Research on Models for the shipbuilding industry will also be built.

The plans for green plots and recreational equipment have been the least precise. Certainly the whole belt along the shore and some of the old cemeteries will be adapted and special recreational areas will be set up in the forests adjoining the city. But will the Central Park, which was planned to be between Oliwa and Sopot and to serve not only Gdańsk but the whole municipal complex, really be made? This park, located almost in the middle of the "Gd" complex, on an area offering exceptional views and good communication service was to contain much rest, sports and entertainment equipment. A large sports stadium was planned to meet the

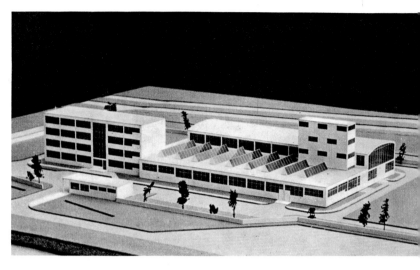

The Institute of Water Tectonics of the Polish Academy of Sciences will obtain new premises in Oliwa

The building of the Flow-Measuring-Machines Institute will be erected in Wrzeszcz

The Maritime Electric Engineering Institute will also receive new premises

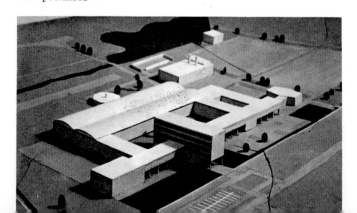

needs of the whole urban combine and it would, of course, require efficient communication service. All these plans were attacked by those who advocated using these grounds for a complex of residiential developments. The next few years will show which conception wins.

To make sure the city and the whole complex will develop harmoniously, it is necessary to develop technical and communication equipment simultaneously. This work will be conducted according to fixed principles that have been discussed previously and are contained in the plans. Further studies and designs will introduce improvements and exactness into the plan; they will also have an influence on the order in which the individual investments are realized. Since more and more goods are expected to be transported by lorry, soon a major problem may be the building of appropriate roads leading to the ports and industrial districts, which by-pass the city.

Technical and economic analysis of communication and engineering problems may influence the di-

rection in which the municipal organism will be developed.

Undoubtedly, the port and large industry will develop towards the north-east and the east for only there can the proper conditions be found. On the other hand, the direction of development of the residential districts may vary: in the Orunia-Pruszcz fragment along the electric railway, in the region of Chełm-Ujeścisko, which is near the centre of town but has a communication problem difficult to solve, or finally on the western hinterland of the municipal complex. The idea of building a shopping centre appropriate to the greatly increased traffic, on the site of the old airport, seems interesting, especially in face of the growing demand for services and of the great development of the whole municipal complex.

Isn't the picture sketched here too far-fetched? Are the forecasts of such a great development of Gdańsk justified? This problem should be discussed on a wider background.

The development of a city is determined by

The centre of Gdańsk by night. Twenty-four years ago there was nothing but ruins and rubble here. This should be kept in mind if one wishes to figure what changes the next quarter of a century will bring

political, economic and social as well as geographical and technical conditions. Their harmonious or contrasting influences decide the development, the stagnancy of decline of cities. Then let us have a brief look at these influences.

The increase in industrialization will require an increase in trade exchange with many countries which, in turn, means that shipbuilding and ports will develop immensely. Already today, the number of four or even five million DWT is mentioned in connection with the plans to develop the merchant marine and if this seems too fantastic, it would be worth recalling that our present fleet of 1,9 million DWT seemed no less a fantasy in 1946 when we had only 120.000.

Industry will be developed along the great rivers, especially the Vistula, with of course the exception of raw material regions. This process has already been started. Nowa Huta, Tarnobrzeg, Sandomierz, Puławy, Wyszogród, Płock, Włocławek, Toruń, Bydgoszcz, Świecie — these are the most important. Locating industry along the Vistula will guarantee water, so necessary for technological purposes, and at the same time, it will relieve the railways by making use of water transportation. Over a dozen dams and hydroelectric plants, together with a system of sluices, will be built on the Vistula to render it more efficient and also for protection against floods. Building on the cascade of the lower Vistula has already begun.

Therefore, the Vistula is becoming the economic axis of Poland, and Gdańsk lies at its mouth. Can these facts fail to have an influence on the fate of the city? Even this is not all. Before this book reaches the reader, more than 500 kilometres of railway line will be electrified connecting Silesia with Gdańsk and Gdynia, thus rendering transportation more efficient along this route.

The factors that will be decisive for the further development of the Gdańsk urban combine are: the general development of town-planning and the industrialization of the country, the concentration of a large part of the new industrial plants on areas that are economically dependent on the Gdańsk-Gdynia complex, the improvement and development of communication connections and, finally, the navigational and technical assets of the ports: lack of slime obstruction, the smallest per cent of ice in winter and the great depths.

Thus, there is no reason to fear a lack of economic basis for the development of the city. On the contrary, it may become necessary to slow down the development and direct it properly in order to avoid hypertrophy of the municipal body. Of course, it is not a question of slowing down the development of the urban combine that is now being shaped, but of giving it a proper spatial structure. This is a problem beyond the scale of Gdańsk itself and is one of the main problems of regional planning.

One thing is certain: never in its history had Gdańsk such advantageous conditions for development; the only problem is to make effective use of them.

Jacket, cover and graphic layout:

WALDEMAR ŻACZEK

Polish Editors:

EWA MUSZYŃSKA, EWA TRZECIAK

Technical Editor:

KATARZYNA MACHOWSKA

Translated by:

JOANNA INFELD-SOSNOWSKA

This book has also been published in Polish and German

*This is the one thousand two hundred twenty-second publication
of Interpress Publishers*

PHOTOGRAPS BY

J. Bułhak: p. 87, 89, 95, 112; J. Ciemnołoński: p. 18, 24, 57, 67, 68, 70, 71; R. Ciszek: p. 212; W. Czajkowski: p. 87 × 2; W. Gruszkowski: p. 95; Z. Kosycarz: p. 17, 43, 98, 114, 125, 139, 159; S. Kruszyński: p. 84; E. Kupiecki: p. 13, 20, 22, 25, 26, 28, 29, 33, 35, 41, 44, 45, 46 × 2, 47 × 2, 48, 49, 50, 51, 52, 53, 54, 55 × 2, 56 × 2, 57, 61, 62, 63, 67, 103, 110, 111, 113, 115, 116, 118, 119, 120, 138, 142 × 2, 143, 145, 146 × 2, 147, 151, 152, 154, 158, 160 × 2, 165, 167, 168, 169, 171, 172, 173, 174, 175 × 2, 178, 180 × 2, 183 × 2, 184, 187 × 2, 189, 192 × 2, 193, 194 × 3, 195, 197 × 3, 203; K. Lelewicz: p. 111; R. Lewicki: p. 213 × 3; M. Murman: p. 12 × 2, 34, 43, 45, 48, 54, 58, 64, 69 × 2, 101, 105, 132, 144, 155, 186, 188, 204, 214; E. Pepliński: p. 10, 22, 27 × 2, 31, 32 × 2, 33, 34, 36, 43, 58, 59 × 2, 62, 68, 69, 75, 76, 82 × 2, 109 × 2, 112, 117, 118, 122, 123, 131 × 2, 132 × 2, 133, 134 × 2, 138, 139, 140 × 2, 141 × 2, 150, 153 × 2, 155 × 3, 158, 159, 160, 164, 166 × 2, 168, 170, 171, 172 × 2, 173, 174, 175, 178 × 2, 179 × 2, 181, 182, 183 × 2, 186 × 2, 188, 189 × 2, 196, 200 × 2, 201 × 2, 202 × 2, 203, 206, 209 × 3, 212; B. Szermer: p. 28; J. Uklejewski: p. 43, 88, 96 × 2, 97, 110, 114, 117, 122, 123, 124, 130, 150, 159, 182, 192, 207 × 2, 208; R. Wyrobek: p. 2, 26, 30, 38, 39, 40, 41, 51, 57, 60 × 3, 66, 67 × 2, 72 × 2, 74 × 2, 75, 88, 89, 116.
Collections from which Photographs were taken Archives of Construction-Research Centre of Ship Industry: p. 161; Archives of Voivodship Urban Workshop: p. 104; Central Photographic Agency: p. 80 (C. Langda), 81 (Z. Matuszewski), 83 × 2, 87 94 × 2, 128 (J. Uklejewski); Gdańsk Shipyard: p. 90, 128, 129.

PRINTED IN POLAND

Illustrations printed by:
ZAKŁADY WKLĘSŁODRUKOWE RSW PRASA — WARSZAWA

Text and cover printed by:
PRASOWE ZAKŁADY GRAFICZNE RSW „PRASA" — WROCŁAW